Megatraumas

Megatraumas
America at the Year 2000

Governor Richard D. Lamm

HOUGHTON MIFFLIN COMPANY/BOSTON 1985

Library of Congress Cataloging in Publication Data

Lamm, Richard D.
Megatraumas: America at the year 2000.

Includes index.
1. Economic forecasting — United States. 2. United States — Economic conditions — 1981– . 3. United States — Politics and government — 1981– . 4. Social prediction — United States. 5. United States — Social conditions — 1980– . I. Title.
HC106.8.L35   1985   338.5′443′0973   85-10692
ISBN 0-395-37912-1

Printed in the United States of America

V 10 9 8 7 6 5 4 3 2 1

The epigraph on page vii is from *The Third World War: August 1985* by General Sir John Hackett et al. Copyright © 1978 by General Sir John Hackett, Air Chief Marshal Sir John Barraclough, Sir Bernard Burrows, Brigadier Kenneth Hunt, Vice-Admiral Sir Ian McGeoch, Norman Macrae, and Major General John Strawson. Reprinted by permission of Macmillan Publishing Company, New York.

Some of the material in this book has appeared, in slightly different form, in *The Futurist, The New Republic, The Humanist,* and *Vital Speeches of the Day.*

"The Time of Peace," by Richard D. Lamm, is reprinted (in slightly different form) by permission from *The Christian Science Monitor.* © 1985 The Christian Science Publishing Society. All rights reserved.

To my children, Scott and Heather,
and to a future that can still be changed

There is a nice story of a political prophet in Munich in 1928, who was asked to prophesy what would be happening to the burghers of his city in five, fifteen, twenty and forty years' time. He began: "I prophesy that in five years' time, in 1933, Munich will be part of a Germany that has just suffered 5 million unemployed and that will be ruled by a dictator with a certifiable mental illness who will proceed to murder 6 million Jews."

His audience said: "Ah, then you must think that in fifteen years' time we will be in a sad plight."

"No," replied the prophet, "I prophesy that in 1943 Munich will be part of a Greater Germany whose flag will fly from the Volga to Bordeaux, from northern Norway to the Sahara."

"Ah, then you must think that in twenty years' time, we will be mighty indeed."

"No, my guess is that in 1948 Munich will be part of a Germany that stretches only from the Elbe to the Rhine, and whose ruined cities will recently have seen production down to only 10 percent of the 1928 level."

"So you think we face black ruin in forty years' time?"

"No, by 1968 I prophesy that real income per head in Munich will be four times greater than now, and that in the year after that 90 percent of German adults will sit looking at a box in a corner of their drawing rooms, which will show live pictures of a man walking upon the moon."

They locked him up as a madman, of course.

— from General Sir John Hackett et al.,
The Third World War: August 1985

Acknowledgments

I'd like to acknowledge Garrett Hardin and Pete Peterson, two people who I believe have a foreboding sense of where the world is going and both of whom spend considerable time fighting to prevent it from happening.

Of course, John Naisbitt deserves special mention. The title of my book, *Megatraumas,* was inspired by his *Megatrends* (Warner Books, 1982), a book that enlarged the screen through which many of us view contemporary events.

I also thank Hunter Lovins of Aspen, Colorado, who read and critiqued the manuscript for this book; Carse Pustmueller, who was extremely helpful on the section called "Requiem for the Forests"; and Leonard Slosky, who helped me on a number of scientific and technical details. I am grateful to Parry Burnap and Barbara O'Brien for their help in research and to Shirley Feller for keeping my life together while I both ran the state and finished this book.

A final note: The statistics for 1984 that I have used in this book are from the sources cited. The year 2000 statistics were either extrapolations or I have assumed the continuation of the 1984 statistics until the year 2000. Thus, in many instances, the current statistics, however shocking, are not presumed to get worse. In the case of inflation, I assume a continuation of the last fifteen years' inflation rate.

Contents

Megatraumas

Prologue

Every society presumes a stable future. That vision may be one of continuing progress or unchanging status quo, but it is almost always a comfortable one, almost never a prognosis of troubled times to come. It is contrary to our natural instincts and our psychic well-being to forecast negative change. Progress is assumed to be our inheritance and a better tomorrow our birthright.

History is often very hard on such illusions. In the large view, it is gratifying to observe how much stability and progress we have had over the past five hundred years. But while progress has been the rule, it is not a guarantee. In many particular instances, it is striking to see how often cataclysmic change has shattered lifestyles, mores, institutions, and even whole societies.

At the dawn of the rather mild winter of 1913–14, few people realized that such change lay just months ahead. Kaiser Wilhelm ruled in Germany; his cousin Nicholas was the czar of Russia; his cousin George was the king of England and ruler of a world empire; the elderly Franz Josef presided over an autumnal Austro-Hungarian Empire. Each was supported by a powerful, rich, and privileged aristocracy. In the family of Europe, only France was a republic — but a quite proper and bourgeois one. Had anyone suggested a radical change in a system of nations so alike in government, social structure, and outlook, he would have been hooted. Had he predicted that two generations in these countries would fight two wars that would kill sixty million people, would overthrow kings and empires, would create a communist Russia, and would deeply alter the future for even the victor nations, he would have been locked up.

It is my contention that the 1980s are a threshold to more enormous historical changes — economic, demographic, ecological, and sociological. The forces for that change have been gathering, but we have failed to see them, or have underestimated them, or have misread them. American optimism and self-confidence have always run so deep that we have never had a talent for precognitions of evil. God gave to our dynamic and ambitious forefathers a continent covered with a foot of the best topsoil; most of our history has been hard on cynics and pessimists. But, as Emerson once said, "Events are in the saddle and ride mankind." The distant thunders warn us of storms.

The view of the future we tend to accept as the natural one is largely based on scientific advance: the information age and the computer revolution, the green revolution in agriculture, the biological revolution that is being created in our laboratories. Our optimism for the future is almost a mirror image of our leading-edge technology. Computers are so cheap that almost anybody can own one, and fiber optics can transmit the contents of an encyclopedia around the world in seconds — so progress is right on schedule. We tend too often to look at the miracles of communication and science and extrapolate that all is well with the world. It is not. Our basic, long-term problems are not being solved — they are being covered over. The future, in fact, is much bigger, darker, and more problematical than anything our bright new technology can dominate.

I believe that America is heading into an era of multiple traumas. For the past fifteen years, our economy has been staggered by a number of external shocks and internal inadequacies. The United States is now a debtor nation. A long-term continued growth of the economic pie, which is so necessary to democracy, is simply not happening. The average American made less money — adjusted for inflation — in 1983 than he did in 1973. Nineteen eighty-four, while posting record economic growth, was a year of recovery built on the quicksand of record deficits. In the early days of my career, political efforts to redistribute some percentage of the national wealth were favored by a growing economic pie. Now that the pie has remained the same size — if not grown smaller — we still try to divide fairly by readjusting the size of the shares.

At the same time, we are not doing enough to restart our economic growth. Have we forgotten such a fundamental truth as the fact that a nation's wealth is its productive capacity — a capacity constituted of a willingness to work hard, to sacrifice, to acquire education and skills, and to invest in tomorrow? That is the part of productive capacity that comes from morale. The other part is the plant, the actual wealth-creating machinery — and both have grown rusty in America.

Our successful rivals among industrial nations have spent on research and development while we have scrimped. They train engineers while we train lawyers. We spend money on doctors and overbuilt hospitals and they spend money on health. The engineers they graduate go to work in the domestic economy to build better exports while 40 percent of our engineers and scientists work at building a defense system.

These countries take an ever-greater share of the world market away from us. They build factories while we build opulent homes. They have pre-empted the leadership in technological innovation in many areas. Their exports grow while our imports grow. They emphasize responsibilities when we emphasize rights. They invest in their future as we mortgage ours. They save and add to their national wealth; we spend and dissipate our national wealth.

The United States is a nation in liquidation.

Even as we have let our economy falter, we have built up incredible demands against it — future social costs and promises that cannot possibly be met. We are deferring, avoiding, or ignoring our problems. Borrowing on the future to sustain a lifestyle we can't afford and neglecting our economic machine is like sowing a minefield through which we must eventually walk. We will not step on every potential mine, but it would be a miracle if we got very far into the twenty-first century without stepping on some of them.

Our borders keep no determined illegal entrants out, and Spanish-speaking immigrants, both legal and illegal, make up by far the majority of U.S. immigration. Demands for a bilingual society are accelerating, and the United States will soon have two frustrated and potentially disruptive minorities. I predict that these demographic changes will be profoundly destabilizing. The birthrate south of our border will haunt us into the indefinite future.

I am not saying that all of the traumas foreshadowed in this book will actually happen. They will not. It is my purpose to describe some of the more ominous trends and to show how they can, if continued, lead to trauma. I am talking about an increasingly vulnerable society, but I am also addressing a nation that, I hope, is sound enough in mind to correct some great follies. The challenge of public policy is to set a sane course between blind optimism and groundless gloom, to be able to define problems and, ergo, define their solutions. We must differentiate between instant political gratification and where our true long-term interests lie. We must think less of today and more of tomorrow.

In the past twenty years of stewardship, my generation of politicians, business leaders, scientists, economists, engineers, and educators has let America lose its lead. Indulgent toward selfishness in the present and only too willing to contract for bills that come due in the future, we have been poor trustees of our nation. On the tablet of history, we will have to confess that "it happened on our watch." In biblical terms we have been "prodigal parents."

Jacob Bronowski, in *The Ascent of Man,* said, "In every age there is a turning point, a new way of seeing and asserting the coherence of the world . . . Each culture tries to fix its visionary moment, when it was transformed by a new conception, either of nature or of man." It is my thesis that we must develop a new way of "asserting the coherence of the world." We can change our course in time.

Thus, despite my nickname of "Governor Gloom," I see this as an optimistic book. I believe that anything predictable in human affairs is preventable. I offer this book not as a prediction of what inevitably must be but as a warning of what might be.

PART ONE

The Facts of Life
in A.D. 2000

The State of the Union in the Year 2000

Following the final disarray of the twelve years of Republican domination, 1980–1992, and one undistinguished Democratic presidency, 1992–1996, Susan J. Hesperus was elected the first woman President of the United States. By the year of her election, the mood of the country was not yet desperate, but it could be described as anxious. The Reagan and Bush terms had been muddled ones, with periods of recession followed by spurts of recovery, but there began to be a general sense among the people that the permanent trend was downhill. Smokestack America, so heavily hit in the mid-1980s, continued to decline, with only a few new computer-run and robot-worked industries thriving. "Twenty-first-century" industries manufacturing high-tech and biologically engineered products employed fewer and more highly skilled workers. The U.S. trade deficit continued to expand and the federal deficit to explode. Neither party had solutions that worked. The clouds on the horizon were very dark.

President Hesperus' first term produced a certain amount of viewing with alarm and some Band-Aid measures to help the economy, cut the deficit, and reduce unemployment. Each cycle of economic downturn was deeper than the last and needed more monetary stimulation to correct. Structural deficits, structural unemployment, and continuing inflation plagued the nation.

The country, without any great enthusiasm, and by a 1.5 percent margin, chose to continue her in office by the election of the year 2000. It was probably less a positive vote than a negative vote against the Republican conservative candidate, Representative Jack Kemp, who was too much identified as a cheerleader for supply-side economics and the Reagan and Bush administrations.

Although not many people seemed acutely conscious of it, by the end of the twentieth century the dark clouds had moved from the horizon to nearly overhead. And, in the course of sixteen years, they had developed into the blackest, most threatening thunderheads since the winter of Valley Forge.

President Hesperus *was* acutely conscious of the gathering storm. Immediately after her re-election, she sent out a directive to all departments, agencies, and bureaus to furnish her with reports. These were not to be the usual summaries and statistical compilations. Her memo said, "I want to read a position paper; I want it to be a thoughtful essay; I want it to reflect your responsibility toward the world as you see it. And I want it to be absolutely honest and realistic." Along with these reports, she gathered a number of other relevant documents from diverse sources.

She was preparing what was to be perhaps the most gloomy — and yet the most candid — State of the Union Message in the history of the Republic. Her Chief of Staff forwarded the reports and documents to her with this warning:

"Per your instructions, some of these are situation memos and others are examples of speeches given by your Cabinet that will allow you to evaluate their continued effectiveness. But, more important, these memoranda catalogue the problems facing your administration. Never in history has an American President confronted so heavy a burden of deferred problems. You may take solace in the fact that you inherited them and are not the cause. Nevertheless, they are now your problems. When you move into a house, at some point you become responsible for its inadequacies. You were re-elected to solve these issues."

These were some of the heterogeneous papers, articles, speeches, and memoranda she collected as the raw material from which she would derive the ideas for her speech.

The Economy

Now that the terms of the trade are turning against the "developed" countries in favor of the "developing" countries, how will the people of the "developed" countries react?

They are going to find themselves in a permanent state of siege in which the material conditions of life will be at least as austere as they were during the two world wars. The wartime austerity was temporary; the future austerity will be perennial, and it will become progressively more severe. What then?

When the peoples of the "developed" countries are forced by events to recognize the inexorability of the new facts, their first impulse will be to fight back. And since they will be powerless to assault other "natives of nature," they will assault one another. Within each of the beleaguered "developed" countries, there will be a bitter struggle for the control of their diminished resources.

— Arnold Toynbee, 1974

Speech by the Secretary of the Treasury to the U.S. Chamber of Commerce April 15, 2000

The President has asked me to use this forum today to respond to some of the criticism she has been getting. She objects to the resolution of your organization opposing her plan to issue a new currency to replace the dollar. She strongly believes that neither the Chamber of Commerce nor the general public understands the pressure that she's under and the options that she's faced with. This is the first presidency of the twenty-first century, and it would be nice to think that we could start this century unencumbered by past mistakes. But you must understand that each president inherits the mistakes of his or her predecessors. This isn't a kind of political checkers where we can start a new game when we want to. Every four or eight years a new man or woman steps into the stream of time and plays the pieces that were put into position by previous presidents. We are thus controlled by the dead hands of past politicians and we must live with their mistakes, grapple with their institutions, cope with their inflation, and suffer under the hate and distrust that their foreign policies have engendered.

We've had a succession of presidents who have purchased temporary tranquility at the expense of the future. Every president since the 1960s campaigned for a balanced budget and came into office with the best of intentions. Yet they all failed to balance the federal budget. Ronald Reagan, who complained the most vigorously about the unbalanced budget, accumulated more deficits in five years than his thirty-eight predecessors did in one hundred ninety-two years. Government has been a giant pyramid scheme, a chain letter to the future, and the problem that this administration faces is that the future is *now*. "Political tomorrow" has arrived. This isn't 1980 or 1985 or even 1990; this is the year 2000, and we live with a legacy of staggering political malpractice on the part of both political parties.

The Bible says that where there is no vision, the people perish. This nation has not had any visions, but instead has been governed by a series of myopic decisions on the part of almost every sector. It isn't only the politicians. The character of the people of this society is as important as the characters we elect to office. It is not only the politicians but the public that has failed to meet the test of our times. Workers' time horizon has been the next paycheck, businessmen's has been the next quarter, politicians' has been the next election. But the true test of any society, of any public policy, is its sustainability. It is my contention that we have not been building a sustainable society and that is the reason for the draconian measures this administration has had to adopt.

Let us first examine the whole question of national wealth. This country has been allowing its wealth to hemorrhage away. When I first assumed public office in 1974, more than twenty-five years ago, this nation had a $9 billion trade surplus. By 1984, it had turned into a $130 billion trade deficit. In 1970, the United States produced 40 percent of the world's gross product. By 1980, it was down to 30 percent and continued to fall after that. In 1970, we were unmistakably first in average per-worker income. By

1980, we were fourth in per-worker income. The United States made the mistake all great empires of history have made. We assumed that it would last forever. We took our prosperity for granted, believing that God was on our side and would protect us from harm. We should have listened to the important words of a wise man who said, "Of the world's known civilizations, the majority have died. Not from the enemy activity, but from the decay from within, and the progression has always been the same: from bondage to spiritual faith, from spiritual faith to great courage, from great courage to liberty, from liberty to abundance, from abundance to apathy, from apathy to dependence, and from dependence, once again, into bondage."

It is not enough for a nation to have a handful of heroes. What we need are generations of responsible people. Heroes are important, but they cannot be a substitute for a society of reliable people who steadfastly place the public interest before their own private interest. We reap what we sow, and a nation that has forgotten how to work hard, how to obey the law, how to sacrifice for the national destiny, is not a nation that can be sustained for any great period of time.

I know the bank controls and credit controls that we have instituted are unpopular, along with our confiscation of all precious metals in private hands. But you must understand that we had no alternative.

In 1985 the United States turned from a creditor nation into a debtor nation. Today we are not only the world's largest debtor nation, we owe more than all the developing nations put together. The world, much of it in poverty, is loaning the United States money to continue its extravagant lifestyle. We thus have two debt crises on our hands: first, the uncollectable funds we have loaned the Third World; second, the very collectable funds we have borrowed from the rest of the world to finance our deficits and sustain our economy. We are the authors of our own economic crisis.

You really must understand how much change I have seen just in my political lifetime. When I graduated from college in 1967, most new cars sold for between $3500 and $5000. My wife and I bought a brand new Volkswagen for $1800. The average single-family home sold for less than $15,000. Gasoline was about thirty cents a gallon and gold was selling for $32 an ounce. Between 1967 and 1984, gasoline prices rose 450 percent. The average home tripled in value and precious metals appreciated 1200 percent. The dollar lost 70 percent of its value between 1967 and 1984.

In the sixteen years between 1984 and the year 2000, we saw the dollar lose another 80 percent of its value. Today, in the year 2000, the 1967 dollar is worth five cents, and it continues to deteriorate even as I speak. Who could conceive then that today our average *monthly* salary would be $20,000, and that the price of the average single-family home would be $800,000?

That is not the fault of this administration. We just have to live with the mistakes of the past and try to control their consequences. Politicians in previous times, for example, budgeted $200 billion deficits "as far as the eye could see." We realized that Argentina, Brazil, and many other Third World countries couldn't pay their debts, but we did not tie this fiscal foolishness into the prices that we had to pay for our goods and commodities. We loaned $600 billion to underdeveloped countries that we knew were already deeply in debt. We Americans are suckers for good news. As Adlai Stevenson said, "Given the choice between disagreeable fact and agreeable fantasy, we will choose agreeable fantasy." The public was fed political pabulum rather than reality, and consequently, this administration has had to take some drastic measures.

I do not like the idea of suspending civil liberties or the imposition of martial law, but the inflation riots of last year left us with no alternative. This administration didn't cause the inflation; we inherited it. America ended up paying for the 1970s oil crisis three times: once when oil went from $3 a barrel to $30; again when inflation caused by OPEC robbed us of our buying power; and the third time when the Arabs deposited their new resources in our banks, and we lent them to countries who couldn't pay us back. It would be funny if it wasn't so tragic. But actions like that caused the hyperinflation with which we now must deal. Martial law is the least onerous of our choices. Hyperinflation is to politics what gasoline is to fire. Hyperinflation preceded Hitler's Germany, Lenin's Russia, and Mussolini's Italy. We are taking away freedom in the name of freedom.

Arnold Toynbee also warned of the fragility of freedom. He observed:

> Man is a social animal; mankind cannot survive in anarchy; and if democracy fails to provide stability, it will assuredly be replaced by some socially stabilizing regime, however uncongenial this alternative regime may be. A community that has purchased freedom at the cost of losing stability will find itself constrained to re-purchase stability at the price of sacrificing its freedom. This happened in the Graeco-Roman world; it could happen in our world too if we were to continue to fail to make democratic institutions work. Freedom is expendable; stability is indispensable.

It is this administration's contention that that is exactly what has happened. An early French philosopher said that "freedom is the luxury of self-discipline," but we did not turn out to be a disciplined people, we did not have disciplined politicians, and we did not have a disciplined political system. We became accustomed to instant gratification, and the glue that held us together as Americans simply became unstuck.

At the same time that our national economy was stagnant, the debts against that national economy increased geometrically. Neither political party had the backbone to stabilize the national spending. The Democrats refused to acknowledge that our domestic programs were out of control and growing by unsustainable rates (for instance, Medicare and Medicaid rose all during the 1970s and early 1980s at 17 or 18 percent a year) and the Republicans refused to recognize that military spending was out of control. The military paid $600 for goods available in local hardware stores for $7. Neither party practiced what it preached or preached what it practiced. And this administration is now left with a national austerity program that we think is our only alternative. Medicare accumulated a deficit of more than $300 billion between 1983 and 1995. And we've had to rescue the Social Security system again. Again, we didn't listen to the warnings. The intermediate assumptions of the Social Security Administration on the actuarial soundness of Social Security, for instance, in 1983, were that there would be only 5.5 percent unemployment by 1995 and a low rate of inflation, that the United States was going to have a rather dramatic increase in its birthrate, and that there would be no substantial increase in life expectancy in the United States. In an almost perverse manner, every one of those assumptions has proven false. Social Security has taken an unacceptably large portion of the worker's paycheck and has certainly accounted for the intergenerational antagonism that has been so plaguing this country for the last fifteen years.

Military pensions and federal civil service pensions were equally unsustainable. They were gifts from generous politicians who purchased present popularity for themselves without regard for the consequences. In 1980, for instance, the $27 billion paid to three million federal military and civil service retirees was almost twice the $15 billion paid to the nine million retirees in the private sector. The federal government in 1982 spent more on the retirement of its employees than it did on *all* its programs for the needy. In that year, the civil service retirement system alone cost $31.4 billion, while the combined total for food stamps, housing assistance, and welfare was $26.9 billion. We attacked the poor, but we didn't have the courage to attack the everyday "you-and-me" subsidies that were really running up the national debt.

Our health care system was also clearly out of control. Again, we myopically failed to see that medical science was rushing us toward a day when we would be faced with the fact that our hospitals were filled with ill people whose physical existence could be prolonged almost indefinitely, but whose quality of life had become intolerable. The cost of this technological torture in the name of health care undercut our economy. We now have a great medical system sitting atop a shattered economy.

Looking back on these mistakes with the wisdom of hindsight, you can see how politicians were able to defer their problems, leaving them to the next generation of politicians. They were essentially faced with three alternatives in dealing with the economy: (1) they could commit political suicide by eliminating sacred spending programs; (2) they could commit political suicide by doubling taxes; or (3) they could start the printing presses and destroy the future by ignoring the problem. As Charlie Brown in "Peanuts" said, "There is no problem so big you can't run away from it." That's what politicians did all through the 1980s and 1990s.

It is understandable, though not excusable, that they might choose to do so. In 1984, for instance, to pay off one year's worth of government debts (the 1984 deficit), each man, woman, and child in the United States would have had to come up with $800 in additional taxes. In other words, to really have pay-as-you-go government, taxes would have had to almost double to offset just 1984's budget deficit, with the tax bill being an extra $3200 for a family of four. By 1989, annual interest on the national debt was $750 per person. Caught between the inability to say no to social programs and the inability to say yes to new taxes for them, the politicians debased our money, ran up massive federal deficits, and ignored the consequences. The blind led the bland.

A society ultimately becomes what it invests in. Capital is the stored flexibility that we have available to meet the future. A nation can print money, but it can't print capital. Capital is real wealth. How we spend it is more than just an important issue. In many cases, it is *the* important issue. A society that does not maintain its investment, or that invests in the present at the expense of the future, or invests in superfluous or nonessential items rather than productive capacity soon finds that it doesn't have a future. The future isn't something that we inherit. It's something that we create by our choices. Maybe we didn't see that earlier, but this administration has been mugged by reality.

Our predecessors made multiple mistakes. Again with the wisdom of hindsight, let me try to list some of them:

1. We assumed continued prosperity. We took for granted a rising level of income and shunned the reinvestment and hard work that our international com-

petitors did not shrink from. They prospered while we
declined. Freedom, democracy, and abundance are not
ironclad guarantees. In fact, they are the historical exceptions, not the rule. Progress is a challenge, not a
promise.

2. We didn't control our systems. We didn't reform our
   health care systems, our pension systems, or any of our
   federal programs until it was too late. We paid Social
   Security to rich retirees, farm subsidies to rich corporate farmers, veterans' benefits to wealthy vets, Medicare to retired doctors, civil service and military pensions to triple dippers, and unemployment to the
   deliberately idle. We dissipated our store of national
   wealth so painfully built up over two hundred years.

3. We didn't control our immigration. The melting pot,
   like any pot, was finite. And although we had entered
   the era of the static economic pie, we accepted massive
   new numbers of people when we couldn't even find
   jobs for our own. We are criticized by our political
   opponents for not pushing the ten million people who
   escaped the 1991 Mexican Revolution back across the
   border to the People's Republic of Mexico. We now
   have ten Cubas south of our border and it would
   be inhuman to force these refugees back to commun-
   ism.

4. Our elections became bidding contests, rather than
   debates over truth. They were occasions for conveying
   promises rather than challenges and political pabulum
   rather than political reality. A number of people tried
   to warn us, but we ignored them. It was like giving
   blind men flashlights.

5. We didn't pay our own way. We borrowed from the
   future to finance a way of life that clearly couldn't continue. We thought we had a divine destiny, but instead
   we had only a deadly decadence.

6. We didn't secure our resource base. We didn't adequately value our own topsoil, for example; it was disappearing even in the 1960s, 1970s, and 1980s at an alarming rate. And we didn't recognize that our strategic fossil fuel and minerals came from two of the most potentially anarchic areas in the world, the Arabian Peninsula and South Africa. We are now strategically isolated.

7. We let our education system deteriorate. In 1983, a report called "A Nation at Risk" (issued by the National Commission on Excellence in Education) stated simply that the United States in the previous fifteen years had committed acts of unilateral educational disarmament in letting its education system deteriorate. We left our children defenseless.

8. Politicians of both parties acted as if they had a duty to lie. Their constituents rewarded them for protecting them from reality. Truth may be in scarce supply, but it always seems to exceed demand.

This administration is not going to be that way. We are trying to rally people around reality, to force our society to make the hard choices that were never made in the '70s, the '80s, or the '90s.

To survive, we must control our excesses, make all our institutions more responsive and efficient, and examine all our governmental goals to make sure they are realistic and compassionate. We must bring back the virtues that built this country: imagination, sacrifice, restraint, thrift, self-discipline. Government is through making promises that we can't keep; we must now learn to manage scarcity.

So we respectfully reject the Chamber's criticism. It came too late. You should have fought harder back in that Orwellian year, 1984, when there was still time.

Thank you.

Memorandum

To: The President
From: The Secretary of Commerce
Re: The Twilight of America's Economy
Date: December 2000

At your request, Madam President, I will try my best to list the causes of the deterioration of the American industrial machine over the last thirty years. This is a tall order, and I do not mean to fix blame to any sector but rather to set a course for the future.

In the decades after the Second World War, Americans took international trade for granted. We were insulated from foreign competition, endowed with immense natural resources, and had a substantial supply of energy and a huge domestic market.

For a hundred years, from 1870 to 1970, America exported a tremendous amount of goods, ran up substantial trade surpluses, and generally built up a phenomenal stock of wealth.

In the 1970s, however, the terms of trade began to change. America the exporter turned into America the importer. The trade deficit has cost the United States a phenomenal number of jobs, shrunk the nation's industrial base, and crippled our growth potential. By 1984, the trade deficit had accumulated to $130 billion, and it became unmistakably clear that America had a major problem. In fact, America has become the world's largest debtor nation.

A number of individual factors contributed to the problem. One of these was the restrictions on grain sales to the Soviet Union, which reduced the U.S. share of the Soviet grain market from 74 percent to 20 percent. But most of the factors were of a more general nature.

First, for instance, was the overvalued dollar. By accruing federal budget deficits we drove interest rates up, increasing the value of the dollar in money markets. It then took many more yen, francs, or deutsche marks to buy an American dollar and consequently to buy American goods. Thus, our domestic economic policy made the dollars held abroad a currency to be loaned, not spent, and in the process, we made it impossible for many American goods to compete in the international marketplace.

Second, once the world had turned into an international marketplace, many American industries that had not known foreign competition suddenly found they had cutthroat competition at home and abroad. The American textile industry, for example, saw not only South Korea and Singapore but mainland China producing goods at prices they could not meet. In 1984, a skilled worker in China made $400 a year, so Chinese manufacturers could price goods made with American labor out of the world market. Foreign capital is often cheaper than U.S. capital because of subsidization by foreign governments that often also target certain markets and furnish not only low-cost capital but a number of other services such as research and marketing support.

Third, other countries blocked U.S. entry into their markets and dumped many of their goods at subsidized rates on the American marketplace. In a marketplace that was really not free, even the genius of the American free enterprise system could not compete with the large subsidies and protections that governments gave their industries.

Fourth, we did not adequately invest in new plant and equipment. Back in the 1970s and 1980s, which was the crucial turning point of the trade imbalance, Japan invested about 10 percent of its gross national product in new plant and equipment while we were investing approximately 3 percent. By the early 1980s, the United States had the highest percentage of obsolete plants, the lowest percentage of capital investment, and the lowest growth in productivity and savings of any major industrialized society. The nations with the new plants and new machines, those that maintained high productivity and high quality, got both the new and old markets. This obviously undercut our ability to compete, and your administration is now paying the price.

Fifth, we allowed our productivity to stagnate. A nation's productivity is the key to its wealth, and our productivity, which created so much new wealth in the period between 1945 and 1975, leveled off and then decreased. Thus we stopped creating as much new wealth as we had during our high-productivity days.

Sixth, America acquired a reputation for producing shoddy goods. With an irony that defies description, the United States and Japan, in forty years, traded reputations. Where Japan used to have a reputation for shoddy goods that was an international joke, by the 1980s American rental companies reported that cars made in the United States required two or three times more servicing than comparable Japanese cars. A Harvard Business School report showed that an average of seventy defects showed up on American assembly-line goods for every one on a Japanese assembly-line product. During the first year of average use there were seventeen service calls on American-made units for every one on a Japanese-made unit. The United States has not maintained its excellence and now we are paying the heavy price.

Seventh, the production of new patents in that same crucial period of the 1970s and 1980s rose more than 350 percent in Japan while our own fell by 10 percent. New ideas are the wealth of tomorrow and we simply were not doing our job of innovation.

Eighth, we ceased to be hard-minded Yankee traders. The Japanese have long been taking shameful advantage of us. Their nontariff barriers have cheated America for years. Customs procedures have been outrageously time-consuming. Standards are often written by the Japanese that exclude American products, sometimes specifically requiring detailed designs used only by Japanese firms. Certification requirements — such as product safety — are cumbersome and often require inspection of each shipment. The Japanese government subsidizes research and development. The Japanese distribution system is biased against American products; retailers seldom display American products prominently. Then, to add insult to multiple injuries, the Japanese have engaged in industrial espionage in the United States for years. America has allowed itself to be severely cheated and imposed upon in ways that would make our Yankee trader forebears blush with shame.

Ninth, the United States hired lawyers and accountants while Japan hired engineers and scientists. We didn't invest our educational resources any better than we invested our industrial resources.

Tenth, we ran out of cheap oil and other cheap resources that had so boosted our economy. We consumed our one-time inheritance of cheap, abundant natural resources. We treated as income what was really capital.

Economic Darwinism

The real keys to the future of the wealth of nations are (1) who has the highest-skilled and best-motivated work force, the one that is willing to work the hardest and increase productivity the most; (2) who has the best innovative technology and the ability to commercialize it; (3) what country invests the most and most imaginatively in education and research and development; (4) which nation saves the most of its GNP and keeps its plants and equipment the most modernized; and (5) which nation has the best access to resources.

We have found, over the last thirty years, that the nations that are the fittest according to these criteria are the ones that have prevailed. There has been an economic Darwinism at work. The nations that have accumulated the greatest wealth are those that have adapted and specialized to maximize the values just outlined.

The United States has not fared well in this new equation. We found that the higher a nation's wage scale was, the more it was forced to automate and the more jobs were lost; and we soon found we were not the only one that could have mass-production assembly lines. On the contrary, in the wink of a historical eye, we found that other nations with much cheaper labor were able to use our technology to beat us at our own game. In a number of key industries, we have lost or are losing our technological edge and are not meeting the international competition.

Social Darwinism

The economic Darwinism has been accompanied by, and certainly helped cause, a social Darwinism. The United States has lost a substantial portion of its middle class. We have moved much more to a two-class society, with skilled workers reaping the benefits of this technological age and unskilled workers and almost everybody else reaping none. The American Dream is fading.

The restructuring of our economy from a manufacturing base to a high-technology, service-industry base has squeezed out the middle-income jobs that provided hope of social mobility so essential to American democracy. We have lost so many of our well-paid production workers while gaining secretaries, waiters, cashiers, and others who earn substantially less than they would in the vanished production jobs. Over the last fifteen years, only two out of the ten fastest-growing new job categories have required any postsecondary education. Automation, robotization, and computers "deskilled" many tasks and turned former middle-class jobs into high-turnover, low-wage jobs.

We are rapidly becoming a two-class society where, on one hand, the skilled employees are well paid and get substantial fringe benefits, and on the other hand, service workers and unskilled workers have poor-paying and often insecure jobs. Dynamic high-tech industries, for example, have a small percentage of highly paid professionals, but below them are a large number of low-skilled, low-paid workers who are in essentially dead-end jobs.

The result of this dynamic is that the number of people living in poverty has grown over the last thirty years, despite numerous government programs to try to prevent it. The real problem isn't lack of government programs, but that U.S. dominance of the world marketplace has now ended. The economy has shifted a number of jobs abroad and put America's goods at a disadvantage because of the overvalued dollar, and the United States has seen a massive shift from high-paying industrial factory jobs to low-paying and dispersed service jobs that has gravely altered our economy.

In the last twenty-five years, the percentage of new college graduates employed in professional and technical occupations has declined. These job areas did not expand as fast as the supply of graduates. Twenty-five to 30 percent of college graduates are estimated to be underemployed. Ph.D.s and M.B.A.s are driving taxis and doing clerical work.

Madam President, we are now faced with a dilemma. We

reap what we sow, and we are paying for another generation's excesses and are crippled by its myopia. In a couple of generations we went from a great economic power, dominating the world marketplace, to a second-rate economic power.

It is our burden to accept these facts, to learn from them, and to set a new course for the future.

Memorandum

To: The President
From: The Chief U.S. Trade Negotiator
Re: Economic Self-Defense
Date: December 2000

Never in history has a nation lost its geopolitical and economic advantage so fast as the United States did following World War II. From being the undisputed richest nation in the world, with an economy that outperformed all others, we have become a country with a second-rate economy that has lost much of its innovative drive.

This was, to a great extent, our own fault. Irresponsible monetary and fiscal policy created an overvalued dollar; American management rested on its laurels; American labor overreached. I should like to set forth the case that, while the United States has been its own worst enemy, other nations also willingly and deliberately contributed to our loss of economic position. The United States has been victimized by its friends and trading partners and we have refused to adopt the self-defense policies that could have protected us against much of our economic decline.

Most nations of the world felt that the United States was fair game for an ingenious kind of exploitation. The "gang of four" — Japan, South Korea, Hong Kong, and Taiwan — have been the worst, deliberately setting up policies for an import-export imbalance that favored them. We have been shamelessly taken advantage of and we were myopic enough to let it happen.

Let us take Japan as an example. The United States has had numerous trade negotiators, trade missions, President–Prime Minister meetings, and trade agreements, and has received an endless stream of excuses and promises. For twenty years, as the trade imbalance grew, we were promised change "immediately."

To date, the U.S. market share in Japan has not changed an iota. Japan's share of our markets has grown exponentially.

When formal Japanese barriers were removed, informal barriers were enacted. Japanese ingenuity at the bargaining table and in the trade associations has triumphed over all Japanese promises and reassurances.

For almost ninety years, the Japanese have been borrowing or stealing our best ideas, polishing them, and applying them to make better products. In the last two decades, Japanese companies have taken dozens of "Made in America" products, perfected them, and undersold us in Japan, throughout the world, and in the United States.

Let us look at the mechanisms they have used to give themselves an advantage. As a general pattern, the following are the most important kinds of nontariff trade barriers:

- *Lack of transparency.* Many Japanese policies and laws are not formulated in public. Foreign firms have a difficult time responding.
- *Administrative guidance.* Most Japanese government agencies have broad discretionary authority in regulating

business. Foreign firms are at a disadvantage in responding to or participating in decisions.
· *Implementation.* Some policy decisions to reduce trade
barriers have not been implemented.

Some of the most formidable Japanese trade barriers are
these: Although Japan uses some international standards in
setting up import regulations, there is little foreign-com-
pany input when the regulations are written, and foreign
firms learn about new regulations long after their Japanese
competitors. Japanese Customs finds it both slow and difficult to evaluate imports made by the Japanese branches of
foreign companies. In fact, all Customs clearances are cumbersome and goods arriving from abroad are subject to
long, unexplained delays.

Japan, despite enabling legislation in 1979, has never
complied with the widely accepted Import Licensing Code.
The allocation of import quotas and the changing of import
restrictions are mysteries that foreign firms have a difficult
time solving.

The Japanese government has a procurement code that
most of its agencies observe — but there are also a number
of large loopholes. If any given agency wishes to freeze out
the alien suppliers, it can grade all suppliers according to
their financial strength and thus eliminate many non-
Japanese firms; it can give short notice (ten to thirty days)
for procurements; it can procure without making a public
advertisement; it most certainly will eliminate any bid that
is not written in Japanese (with the exception of NTT,
Nippon Telegraph and Telephone).

Japanese protectionist policy is probably best exemplified by the history of the computer and semiconductor
industries from the 1950s to the mid 1970s. Practically all
foreign competition in the field was barred from Japan

while Japanese firms were loaded with subsidies, tax benefits, and government procurements.

Patent registration in Japan is close to absurdity. It may take as long as six years for a foreigner to get a patent. In the meantime, his patent submission is open to the public and available to competitors — and Japanese law does not provide for any discovery process to find out which competitors might have stolen it. Japan, furthermore, has no effective legal protection of trade secrets.

While the United States allows foreigners to invest freely here, the same kind of investment in Japan is limited. Another problem is the closed industrial society — with most major firms interlocked both with each other and, through a web of informal relationships, with government regulators.

Some other highly protected business areas are the trucking, stevedoring, and warehousing businesses; automobile sales; and pharmaceutical licensing for manufacture. Foreign publishers work under one peculiar handicap in Japan — their employees have an extremely difficult time getting a work permit for more than three months.

While Japan is probably an extreme example of the kind of protectionist world in which American exporting industries must make their way somehow, it represents many of the worldwide trends that have victimized the United States and contributed to its economic decline.

Health Care

May you make a million dollars and spend it all on doctors!
— old Middle Eastern curse

Speech by the Secretary of Health and Human Services to the Association for a Better New York February 15, 2000

Thank you for your invitation to speak this morning. It's an honor to be in New York City and addressing the Association for a Better New York. I've had many speaking engagements since being appointed Secretary of Health and Human Services, but this is the first chance I've had to speak to your group and explain the administration's new policies.

This administration's health rationing proposal has caused a firestorm of criticism. We have found, sadly, that we cannot do for everyone all that medical science is capable of doing — that we must draw lines never before drawn. At some point we must say additional public expenditures are not cost effective. We are proposing not funding transplants, artificial organs, or extraordinary procedures for those over sixty-five. We understand the criticism, but I submit we have no alternative. Health care is a public policy bottomless pit. We can never reach the end of demand.

I should like to review the last twenty years with you and show how serious the problem of runaway medical costs has become.

Let us go back to 1983, which I think was our last opportunity to solve this problem by less draconian measures. Health care expenditures were rising at three times the general inflation rate and had already reached ten and a half cents out of every dollar spent in America. That was $355 billion dollars a year, approximately $1 billion a day, $40 million dollars an hour, $12,000 a second. The average American, though he or she seldom knew it, paid $1500 in 1983 for health care, more than he or she paid in individual income tax. Spending by federal and state governments alone was $600 per capita for health care, which was one and a half times the *total* cost of all health care in Britain of $400 per capita. Government expenditures had, since 1965, doubled every four and a half years. During this time we had truly seen an egalitarian health revolution — we had substantially improved the problem of access. We had truly made health care available to enough poor so that in the early 1980s, poor Americans saw a doctor more often than rich Americans.

We had successfully completed one health care revolution, but the sad part of it is that, though egalitarian, it was the most expensive and inefficient health care system in the world. We had made very little progress in preventing disease and promoting health. Although we made heroic efforts to prolong "life" in some individuals, the improvement in our health has been insignificant compared to the increase in the cost of health care. For example, in 1984, Medicare alone paid out $15 billion for the treatment of terminally ill Americans in the last six months of their lives: that's more than the entire gross national product of Bangladesh.

Now, capital is the not-so-secret weapon a society has with which to meet the future. It is always finite. We can either spend it in retooling and reindustrializing our society and rebuilding a first-rate education system, or we can spend it wastefully and inefficiently in ways that drain capital from the productive part of our economy. In 1984,

Chrysler had to produce 70,000 automobiles just to pay its health care costs; $550 of the retail price of an automobile went to health care for Chrysler workers. This partly explains why the United States had such a staggering trade deficit and why it has so rapidly been eclipsed in the international marketplace. The increase in the price of our goods and services contained substantial and dramatically rising health care costs, which helped price American goods out of so many markets.

Now, some argued, back in the 1980s, that this was no problem, that the service sector was rapidly replacing traditional manufacturing and construction as the major growth sector of our economy. Spiraling medical costs were argued to be just one part of the service sector. This is a tragically mistaken notion. If we were all to get cancer tomorrow, the GNP would go up, but that is, both figuratively and literally, not the type of growth we seek! How we spend our limited capital controls whether our children get jobs and what kind of America our grandchildren inherit.

Thus, American health has improved only slightly, while our growing investment in health care costs has crippled the national economy. The growing cost of health care is not just a benign tumor on the national economy. It is an economic cancer that has prevented America's goods from being competitive in the world marketplace. Republican senator Tom Kean warned in 1984, when he was governor of New Jersey, that health care costs were the "Pac Man of his budget," eating up the flexibility that he needed to improve other important sectors of the system. But we didn't listen, we allowed health care costs to increase enormously, both in actual amount and in percentage of the gross national product, taking away capital from other immensely important functions.

Now this administration is left only with hard choices.

John Locke once said, "Hell is truth seen too late." It is our hell to discover this truth too late. If a company raises prices to pay the dramatically increasing health care costs of employees, it can no longer compete with lower-priced foreign products. This nation should have recognized long ago that we cannot continue to spend an increasing percentage of the gross national product on health care, especially when the system has not made us among the healthiest in the industrialized world but, ironically, has tended to do the opposite. For at least the last twenty years, there has been a negative correlation between the number of doctors in each industrialized country and the average life expectancy. Japan had the fewest doctors per hundred thousand people and the longest life expectancy. West Germany had the most doctors and the shortest life expectancy.

Did we really think, back then, that the existing medical care system could or should go on forever? To think so would confuse arithmetic with geometry and is to dramatically misunderstand compound growth rates. French president Valéry Giscard d'Estaing said, shortly before he left office in 1981, "All modern-day curves lead to disaster." That is clearly what happened to health care costs. We didn't make simple corrections early enough, and now the President is faced with nothing but very, very hard choices. Thus our national health rationing proposal.

It should have been apparent, for decades, that a number of things were dramatically wrong with the health care system that contributed to its inefficiency. First, it was estimated that there were between 100,000 and 200,000 excess hospital beds in the United States and that 30 percent of all of the people who were in a hospital bed at any given time were not there for medical reasons. They were often there for the convenience of the doctor or to satisfy provisions in an outdated insurance policy. Translated into the costs incurred, that meant that tens of billions of dollars in hospital expenses could have been avoided. Similarly, there was dramatic evidence of excessive numbers of operations. For instance, in 1984 it was estimated that of the 800,000 hysterectomies performed in one year, fully one-third were unnecessary. Similar statistics were given for a number of other operations.

Second, we were spending too much money out of fear of lawsuits. Doctors and many hospitals, afraid of malpractice suits, often thought they had to administer unneeded tests to leave a paper trail as part of their practice of defensive medicine. The surplus of lawyers in this country — for the last ten years, America has had over two-thirds of all of the lawyers in the world — has added tremendous costs to the health industry.

Third, the United States has been spending too much on the installation of the newest technologies at competing hospitals. CAT scanners and nuclear magnetic resonance devices, for example, lay idle much of the time or were used unnecessarily to recover their cost. There was a dramatic and very costly duplication of facilities that added greatly to our health care expenditure.

Fourth, we were training too many doctors. The number of doctors in our society went from 170 per hundred thousand in 1970 to 190 per hundred thousand in 1984, to, today, more than 200 per hundred thousand. Eighty-five percent of American doctors are specialists, and all of them find some way to earn good livings off the system.

Fifth, we did not recognize that medical science was inventing treatments faster than public policy could pay for them. Hundreds of thousands of dollars were spent on developing the mechanical heart, and we continue to approach blindly the day of the bionic man without asking ourselves who is going to pay for this and how we can afford it. Now this administration has to do something tough to control staggering medical costs.

Sixth, we didn't spend our health care money very wisely. For the last ten years, or longer, the causes of premature death in our society were vastly different from the causes of death generally. The causes of premature death were clearly smoking too much, eating too much, drinking too much, and not wearing seat belts. If we could have reduced cigarette smoking by half, back in the early 1980s, we would have done much more for health in the United States than all of the massive spending programs. Instead we subsidized tobacco products and ignored preventive medicine. We had a "disease care" system rather than a "health care" system.

We have clearly made a Faustian bargain with our health care. The spending on this has given us many miracles of high technology, many beautiful hospitals, and a whole cadre of well-trained doctors. The price that we've paid for this has been a system that grew as an economic cancer until it blocked out other significant sectors of our society and led us to the brink of national bankruptcy.

Nowhere was this more apparent than in the area of death and dying. The United States has, for a long time, been a death-denying culture. In his book *Medical Nemesis: The Expropriation of Health,* Ivan Illich stated, "The medicalization of society has brought the epic of natural death to an end. Western man has lost the right to preside at his act of dying. Health, or the autonomous power to cope, has been expropriated down to the last breath." In an incredible number of instances, miracle machines were used not to prolong life but to prolong dying. We are now capable of maintaining some semblance of life almost indefinitely: we can be kept alive biologically, but long after we have ceased to exist as thinking, feeling human beings.

As one doctor, writing in the *New England Journal of Medicine*, stated so well some twenty years ago: "My personal experience in the practice of neurology for over twenty years is that there is a widespread refusal to acknowledge the suffering and degradation experienced by helpless people permanently maintained with life support systems. The American health care system breeds a mentality of turning away from this consideration, perhaps because it does not acknowledge the reality that there is a time to die."

It is estimated that as much as 30 percent of all Medicare dollars are spent on the last few months of patients' lives. Consequently, a huge percentage of our health care dollars are being spent on patients who have no chance of recovery. Many of these expensive high-technology procedures and machines drain our ability to pay for other medical procedures. The exorbitant cost of high-technology medicine is one of the main factors cited for declining funds for prenatal care and health care for the indigent. We simply did not ask ourselves if the government should spend $100,000 for an operation on a terminally ill person in the last year of life, or, alternatively, give eight thousand children dental care or twelve hundred children immunizations.

Until recently, unlimited medical resources were taken for granted. We had the luxury of an economy in which we did not have to face the moral dilemma of who would not be treated because we did not have the resources to treat everyone. Now we know that we can't afford everything.

We simply did not have the societal maturity to face up to the fact that life is a terminal disease, that each one of us is destined to have an end-stage illness of some kind, and that even a country as wealthy as the United States could not afford to entitle everyone to all the medical care that technology invented without doing significant trauma to other aspects of its economy. How many hearts should we give to a smoker? How many liver transplants can we afford to give to an alcoholic?

We have allowed our great and proper humanitarian desire to preserve life to control our health care decisions, even when the probability of a patient's recovery approaches zero. These futile attempts to add another week or so to the lives of the terminally ill consumed resources that could have, if properly allocated, saved many. Technological immortality has now run right into fiscal reality.

Thus, in some terrible respects, modern medicine has given us not longer life but slower death. By our moral and legal ambivalence and our refusal to confront this last taboo, warm, loving human beings are being condemned to a living death, hooked up to miracles of modern technology that offer them not recovery but a long, drawn-out death.

So the President respectfully rejects your association's criticisms. We did not solve the problem in time to avoid drastic measures. She has had no other choice than to propose a program of national health rationing. It is axiomatic that the earlier you start to deal with a problem, the easier the solutions, but we did nothing. We allowed structural deficits to accumulate, structural unemployment to fester, and structural excesses in our health care system to allocate an unacceptable and unsustainable percentage of our national wealth to health care that was wasteful and inefficient.

Winston Churchill once said, "America can be trusted to do the right thing . . . after it has exhausted all other possibilities." This administration does not have any other possibility because we didn't have the foresight to reform our system earlier. Thus all of our choices are hard ones.

George Bernard Shaw said, "All great truths begin as blasphemies." Infinite needs have finally run into finite resources. If you wanted something less drastic than national health rationing, you should have done something back in 1984.

Memorandum

To: The President
From: The Surgeon General
Re: The Bionic Man
Date: January 20, 2001

We live, Madam President, in the age of the bionic man. Multiple organs are now capable of being transplanted and we have workable and improving artificial organs ready to pass out of the "experimentation" stage and become available to the public at large. Medical science has delivered us a giant step toward bionic immortality.

But it has created for us a moral and economic Frankenstein's monster.

We have no ethical or moral standards as to how we should distribute these organs, and it is becoming increasingly clear that the current system is based on status according to wealth and political connections.

When a technology becomes available in a society, the media and the public demand that it be put to use, even though we have no idea what it is going to cost society and even though neither the medical profession nor society has made an analysis of how cost effective the machine would be. If we invent it or perfect it, we must use it, the theory goes.

We estimate the current demand for heart transplants at 30,000 to 75,000 per year, liver transplants at 10,000, kidney transplants at 20,000, pancreas transplants at 10,000, and angioplasties at 200,000. These transplants cost from $25,000 each (pancreas) to $200,000 each (liver), and each organ recipient will need a yearly prescription of cyclosporin at a cost of $10,000 per year. This list does not even include ear implants for the deaf, cultured skin transplants for burn victims, artificial organs, the implantable defibrillator, or other procedures too numerous to mention.

The genie is out of the bottle with the development of these technologies and we must now establish standards for allocation of these advances. The desperate need for guidelines is underscored by the growing presence of a black market in organs. Third World citizens are selling their kidneys, and other organs that can be furnished only by murder are appearing on the market.

Do we make money the standard of access? It is the historic standard. After all, money has always helped ensure survivability. The *Titanic* survival rate was 97 percent of all female first-class passengers, 84 percent of all female second-class passengers, and 55 percent of all female third-class passengers.

Some argue that just as we limit food aid, so should we limit medical aid. We give the poor access to food stamps but not to our best restaurants, and it is argued that we should furnish a minimum level of standard care to the poor but not offer them the exotic technologies.

Such a decision would seem a moral nightmare.

England rations on the basis of age. There is something somewhat more comforting about that standard, as it doesn't involve money, but in this country organizations of senior citizens have made opposition to this a key plank in their age-discrimination policy.

Should we do individual cost-effectiveness evaluations? Ironically, so much of what medicine does is not "cost effective" in a macro sense.

In 1978, a study examined motor vehicle accidents, cancer, and heart disease and compared the total potential taxes the individuals would have paid if they had not died with the total retirement and medical benefits they would have received if they had lived to their 1978 life expectancy. Interestingly, neither cancer research nor research on heart disease was found to be "cost effective."

An estimated $24.9 billion in future taxes was estimated to be lost because of premature deaths from heart disease in 1978. Had these victims lived to their life expectancy, however, they would have claimed $40 billion in benefits for the aged. Thus, reducing mortality from heart disease puts a significant drain on the U.S. Treasury.

The Treasury also incurred significant costs because of the survival of elderly women owing to cancer research. (Women generally live longer than men, so their cancer survival rate is higher.) Preventing auto accidents had a positive effect only because a majority of the victims of car accidents were young men at the beginning of their productive lives.

In all three cases, however, the federal benefits the individuals would have received were greater than the taxes they would have paid had they survived.

So much for cost-benefit studies.

But we must address the issues raised by our new technologies. If we do not employ cost-benefit ratios, what standard do we use? It is hard to resist such life-giving miracles as transplants and artificial organs when the victims are so visible. The power of the media, therefore, plays an important role in the allocation of resources. But does it give us the right public policy answers?

The money spent on artificial organs could be better spent on many other procedures that benefit far more people and provide the American public better total health. We should direct more resources to prevention and fewer to treatment. But we treat individuals while we prevent only statistics.

The 55 mph speed limit was a great life saver — but we saved statistical lives, not specific ones. There is nobody on whom you can focus a television camera. The thousands of children who would benefit from prenatal care are anonymous, but Baby Fae, whose own heart was replaced with a baboon's, was very specific and very lovable. Before she died, she had become an overnight media sensation.

Thus our hearts — not our heads — allocate our medical resources. Media-driven humanitarianism ends up saving a few specific lives, but it ignores, and we lose, many more anonymous lives because we turn our backs on those we cannot see.

We allow heart transplant patients — usually heavy smokers — to damage their hearts with subsidized tobacco, and we rush to fix them. But we do nothing to stop subsidizing tobacco, little to screen for hypertension, nothing to emphasize the relationship of heart trouble to diet, stress, or lack of exercise. We support the visible "wonders" of health care but ignore the invisible prevention that could save far more lives. It's as if the March of Dimes had thrown all its resources into iron lungs instead of helping Jonas Salk develop the polio vaccine.

If we can't do everything, and we can't, we should spend our money intelligently where it will buy the greatest amount of American health. That would clearly not be on artificial organs for the few but on preventive health care for the many.

I do know that our new technical abilities have outstripped the boundaries of our conventional medical ethics and community standards. In the real world that this administration is trying to confront, we clearly will not be able to give everything medically available to everyone. Simply put, our health care system is making us economically sick.

But, Madam President, we must find a defensible standard before we bankrupt the country.

Tenets of the Eskimo Society

We are an organization founded in 1999 and already a hundred thousand strong. We believe that *we* own our own bodies and that when we are done living we should have the right to effect our own deaths. The state does not own our bodies, our neighbors don't, Medicare doesn't — we do, and we shall fight for legislation allowing us to choose our own end. Like the Eskimo elderly, we seek not to be a burden. We fear not death but the loss of autonomy and personal dignity, especially, but not exclusively, due to terminal illness. We are realistic about death. We all must die. Death is not a tragedy — but dying without dignity, separated from our loved ones in an alien environment, needlessly suffering, is.

We face a new reality not faced by previous generations. The great majority of us will die slow, painful, expensive deaths with great financial and psychological cost to ourselves, our families, and our country. We are often put in

Medicare warehouses (the twentieth-century equivalent of the Elizabethan poorhouse), where many of us will lie in bed for months or years, often paralyzed, comatose, or helpless, and usually in great pain. One-third of us will die of cancer and many of us will be victims of dementing diseases. Modern medicine and technology have made death degrading, painful, prolonged, and even profane. We prefer a quick and painless death to a slow, painful one.

We seek "one more pill" to allow us compassionate control over our own bodies. A slow death is not only degrading but has forced millions into bankruptcy and/or poverty. We don't force life upon our terminally ill dogs or other pets; yet we do on our elderly. Society refuses dying people release, even if they beg to end their suffering. We are daily making sacrifices of prolonged suffering to the new secular god, technology.

We seek "self-determination" as a final "civil right." Suicide is the ultimate self-determination. The Bible tells us that Saul "fell upon his sword," and the early Christians were called martyrs and sainted when they deliberately chose death over betrayal of their religion. We seek the same right and privilege: the understanding that there are some circumstances under which we do not care to live.

We seek more than a "living will." We seek more than a lingering, painful "natural death." A "natural" death often requires months and years of unnatural living. We seek the self-determination to end our lives under conditions that we feel are just and sufficient. We do not think it proper for the state to interfere, with its laws and prejudices, in this final and important right. We demand, for our own sake and the sake of our nation, the right to "timely suicide."

We demand that all hospitals, VA centers, and nursing homes be required to provide the "coup de grâce" pill to those of us who need and desire such help. No hospital or nursing home should be allowed to deny the right of a painless death to any dying human being.

We note that Zeno, founder of the Stoics, stated more than two thousand years ago: "The wise man will for reasonable cause make his own exit from life on his country's behalf, or for the sake of his friends, or if he suffers intolerable pain, mutilation, or incurable disease." After all these years, we as a society are not even to the point where Zeno started. We should have an absolute right to effect our own ends.

We are not trying to impose our views on others. Those who wish to die a slow, painful death should be free to do so. We oppose euthanasia, but we demand the right to suicide by the dying. Some will consider suicide a sin and that is their right. But they should not make it a crime and impose often hopeless torment on the rest of us who choose to follow our own consciences and avoid the degradation and suffering of modern death.

Pensions

Old men must die, or the world would grow mouldy . . .

— Tennyson

Praised be Thou, O Lord, for our sister Death, from whom no
mortal can escape.

— St. Francis of Assisi

Memorandum
For Your Eyes Only

To: The President
From: The Re-election Committee
Re: Intergenerational Conflict
Date: January 2000

The most difficult political dilemma this campaign faces this fall is the rise of intergenerational conflict — that is, the elderly versus the rest of the voters. It is explosive and the outcome in November can depend directly upon how we handle this volatile issue.

Simply put, America's elderly have become an intolerable burden on the economic system and the younger generation's future. In the name of compassion for the elderly, we have handcuffed the young, mortgaged their future, and drastically limited their hopes and aspirations.

The policymakers of the 1960s and 1970s devised themselves golden parachute retirement programs and placed the cost in succeeding generations. They bought themselves homes with low interest rates and pay off those cheap loans with inflated dollars. They set up unsustainable pension systems — in government, in Social Security, and in many cases in private industry, and then they indexed them from the inflation that followed from their own excesses. They placed the bill for all these programs on succeeding generations, who consequently inherited the crippled economy their excesses caused. With a smile and grandfatherly advice, we tell the young to pay for our elderly's Social Security, military pensions, veterans' benefits, Medicare, nursing homes, and so forth. So what if both young parents have to work to support these systems and still earn a living? So what if grandchildren have to suffer because of our overgenerous and unsustainable programs for the elderly? The biblical story of the prodigal son has been turned on its head: we now have the sad but true story of the "prodigal father."

It is easy to see how this problem has developed. In 1970, 20 million Americans were over sixty-five years of age; by 1985, the number had risen to 29.5 million; today it is 39 million. They will number at least 55 million by 2031.

People over sixty-five in 1900 made up 4 percent of the population. It was 12 percent in 1985 and it is 17 percent today. And it is those in this category who vote in the heaviest numbers.

The problem is not going to get any easier. It is estimated that by the year 2040 nearly 20 percent of all Americans, some 50 million, will be sixty-five years or older, and we estimate that 40 percent of the federal budget will be devoted to them.

The increase in the number of aged, combined with our runaway health care costs, has given us the most expensive and fastest-rising aspect of the federal budget. Back in 1980, there were 105 million hospital patient days per year for persons age sixty-five and older; today there are 275 million such days. Adjusted for inflation, the costs of hospital care for the aged have tripled. The costs are not distributed evenly. It is estimated by Medicare that 7 percent of the people on Medicare receive an astonishing 67 percent of all Medicare costs.

This problem is seen particularly with the "old-old." The

United Senior Coalition has accused you of being "insensitive" to their needs (spelled better, "demands"). But political realism requires us to listen to their agenda. This is the fastest-growing bloc of voters and the most volatile. America has a new "minority" group to incorporate into its political spectrum.

In 1950 only about half a million people in the United States were eighty-five or older, but today they number 5,136,000. In fifty years this old-old category has increased 900 percent. Very old women now outnumber very old men by five to two.

In 1980 one-quarter of the old-old were in nursing homes, and that percentage still holds. That means that we have built an average of one new nursing home for a hundred people *every* day from 1984 until today. That has been a staggering burden.

The incidence of dementing illnesses such as Alzheimer's disease roughly doubles every five years after age sixty-five. Thus, 1 percent of those sixty-five years old have a dementing illness; 2.5 percent of those age seventy; 5 percent of those age seventy-five; 12 percent of those age eighty; more than 20 percent of those between eighty-five and ninety; and 40 to 50 percent of those in their nineties. All other chronic diseases show up with increasing frequency.

Veterans are another elderly subgroup that has exploded in numbers. We now have nine million veterans over age sixty-five — three times the number there were in 1984. Two out of every three American men over sixty-five are veterans. We will spend $44.6 billion on military pensions in fiscal year 2000, compared to $1.2 billion spent in 1964.

The real crunch comes in the backlash we have been getting from current workers. These people are understandably growing resentful at the increasing burden placed upon them. An article in *Time* magazine last month,

"Choosing Between Children and Grandparents," gave great insight into the dilemmas faced by many families forced to sacrifice spending for their children because of the burden of the elderly.

In 1980 there were four workers for every retiree, and by 1990 this ratio was three to one. By the year 2020 there will be only 2.2 workers for every retiree. We are heading toward age polarization and the revolt of the young. They will only sacrifice so much for their grandparents.

The dilemma we face in the immediate future is that the generation consisting of those born in the 1940s is starting to retire — just when the smaller numbers of those born in the "birth-dearth" days of the 1960s and 1970s become the working population.

That is the political tightrope we must walk this election.

Memorandum

To: The President
From: The Director of the Office of Management
        and Budget
Re: Pensions
Date: January 20, 2001

We have a crisis of funding for pensions and veterans' benefits that is going to have to be addressed during your second term.

Military Pensions

Military pensions are but one example of the generous decisions made by the previous generation of politicians that were at variance with common sense and that must be brought into line with the realities we now face. The most common retirement age for officers in the United States military is forty-three, and for enlisted men the most common retirement age is thirty-nine. Nine out of ten military pensioners are of working age, and most of these are employed in other jobs and still drawing their retirement benefits. Ninety-three percent of the people who have retired, up to now, did so before the age of fifty, and 26 percent of those retired when they were still in their thirties. Thus the average career soldier receives more than $500,000 ($228,-000 in 1984 dollars) in retirement payments during his or her lifetime, plus free medical care. That would compare with the recent retirement payments to a pensioner in the private sector, which are closer to $70,000 ($37,000 in 1984 dollars). Military pensions are thus six times more lucrative than private pensions for their civilian counterparts.

Military pensions are a very large part of this country's growing defense budget and are one of the rapidly growing sectors of that rapidly growing budget. They totaled $11.9 billion in 1980, rose to $17.2 billion in 1985, and cost $44.7 billion today.

Senator Les Aspin, sixteen years ago when he was on the House Armed Services Committee, stated, "We made a terrible mistake in the early 1970s when we started raising military pay. We should have changed the pension formula, but we didn't; now we're paying the price." That price has increased significantly.

The bill for pensions has shot up six times greater than the overall increase in defense spending over the past twenty years. Retirement programs were 2 percent of the Pentagon's budget in the early 1960s, 6.5 percent in 1983, and 12 percent today.

Four major factors have led to this dramatic increase:

1. The sharp jump in the number of veterans receiving pensions, as a large number of World War II, Korean War, and Vietnam War veterans retired from active duty.
2. The increase in military pay that is the basis for calculating retirement benefits.
3. The fact that all pensions are indexed to cost-of-living increases caused by inflation.
4. The fact that military retirees, along with other Americans, are getting better medical care, living longer, and thus drawing benefits over more years.

Keep in mind that all of the military pensions are totally noncontributory.

Many armed forces personnel leave the military at about the age of forty, take another job and collect both a salary and a military pension for twenty to twenty-five years, then retire and receive triple benefits — (1) from the military pension, (2) from the retirement pension, and (3) from Social Security. If that person goes to work in the civilian side of the federal government, the military retiree can simultaneously receive both a federal salary and a federal pension for twenty to twenty-five years, and then receive two substantial federal pensions for the remainder of his or her life.

The recipients of military pensions fall largely into the upper-income tax brackets. Sixty percent of all military retirement benefits go to the wealthiest one-fifth of all U.S. households. Eighty-three percent of all military pensions go to the top two-fifths of all households. There is no other federal entitlement program that begins to pay such a proportion of its benefits to the most affluent sectors of our population. Conversely, the bottom fifth of the U.S.

households receive only 2 percent of the military pension benefits and the bottom two-fifths of the population receive only 6 percent of those benefits.

Most military retirees are in high income brackets because they don't retire, they take another well-paying job. Two-thirds of those collecting military retirement benefits are working at another job. Twenty-nine percent of officers with the rank of army major, navy lieutenant commander, or above, who retired in 1999 worked for a defense contractor. The government thus pays them a direct pension and an indirect salary. Pensions don't even go to many who fought for our country. Eighty-seven percent of those who enter the armed forces and even most who have been in combat never receive any retirement pay. It is paid to a small group of well-off people, and this inequity cries out for reform.

Military retirement is the second most expensive federal entitlement program coming directly from the general tax revenues. Medicaid is the most expensive, but it covers fifteen times as many beneficiaries. Thus, military retirement programs cost the federal government one-third more than food stamps and twice as much as Aid to Families with Dependent Children (AFDC).

There is no retirement fund to cover these pensions, but like the other federal programs, it is an obligation to be met by future taxpayers. The unfunded liability of military pensions will have to be covered in future years.

Federal Civil Service Pensions

A career civil service worker can retire at the age of fifty-five with no reduction in pension. As in the case of a military person who can retire after twenty years, no matter what age, this policy sticks the taxpayer with decades of inflation-protected payout. The estimate of future costs that are not covered by any kind of retirement fund but will have to be taken out of future federal budgets is now estimated to be above $1 trillion.

It is also estimated that most federal workers ultimately get two pension checks, both fully hedged against inflation — first, a federal civil service pension, and, second, for the four out of five who have worked long enough in the private sector to qualify, Social Security benefits. One in four federal retirees retired on disability under some of the most liberal disability retirement programs ever devised.

One has to realize fully how much these programs are costing the federal government. According to the Congressional Budget Office, Social Security and other programs that have no means test pay out four dollars for every one that goes to means-tested programs such as food stamps and AFDC. If we are really going to reform federal spending, we will have to follow the Willie Sutton theory of robbing banks — "go to where the money is" — and eventually attack these non-means-tested, out-of-control entitlement systems.

Veterans' Benefits

Old soldiers don't "just fade away," as the old saying made famous by General Douglas MacArthur would have it; they stay around for a substantial time to draw benefits from the system.

The retirement of 13 million veterans of World War II, over the last twenty years, has sent the expenditures of the Veterans Administration on health care and income security through the roof. The number of veterans sixty-five and older tripled from three million in 1980 to nine million by the year 2000.

Veterans over sixty-five years of age are shown to have received five times as much health care as those under sixty-five, and World War II veterans already over sixty-five are two and a half times as likely to be collecting disability payments. Under our current programs, the Veterans Administration pays for both service-connected and non-service-connected disabilities.

There were about three million veterans over age sixty-five up until 1981, and then every five years beyond that between four and five million veterans have turned sixty-five. Four million veterans are over seventy-five years of age, a fourfold increase in two decades. The VA is the government's fourth largest spending agency and the third largest employer of federal employees. Even before the explosion in the number of World War II veterans, it ran the largest hospital system in the world.

The VA system cost $8.3 billion in 1983, $9.7 billion in 1986, $15.4 billion in 1990, and $25 billion today.

We have a khaki crisis on our hands.

The Four Myths of the Elderly: White Paper from the American Association of Working People January 2000

The American Association of Working People has been organized to defend the rights of American working men and women. We care about the elderly, but we also care about our children. It is our intention to be both compassionate and realistic. We thus respectfully point out some of the myths being perpetuated by elderly special interest groups who seek to enlarge their own share of limited resources at the expense of the nation and of the working men and women of America.

Myth #1. To be elderly is synonymous with being needy.

It is clear from the national statistics that the elderly are no poorer than the other demographic cohorts of America. In per capita income, adjusted for family size, the elderly are better off than people under sixty-five. Furthermore, two-thirds of the elderly own their own homes without mortgages, and they expend less on most other necessities besides housing except health care.

Thirty years ago the elderly had a higher poverty level, but that has not been true for the last twenty years, and in fact, the elderly population now shows a lower poverty rate than the general population.

Myth #2. America has a social contract that allows us to retire no later than age sixty-five.

Today's retirement age is unrealistic compared to the new realities that this nation faces. In 1935, when the age of eligibility for Social Security was set at sixty-five, the average person was expected to live 12.5 more years. In 1984, the average seventy-two-year-old could expect to live 12.5 more years, and today, in the year 2000, the average seventy-five-year-old can expect to live 12.5 more years. Entry into old age now begins, realistically, no earlier than the age of seventy-two. Today, one-fourth of the people in the United States, more than 74 million, are fifty-five years of age or older. By 2050, one out of four will be sixty-five or older, and in that year 5 percent will be eighty-five or older. Additionally, by the year 2050, there will be thirty-eight elderly people for every hundred of working age, compared to nineteen elderly people per hundred of working age back in 1984. We cannot ignore the biological fact that people are living longer. The age of retirement that made sense in 1935 makes sense no longer.

Additionally, polls show that a large percentage of workers nearing sixty-five would like to continue working, at least part time, and it is the position of this organization that it is senseless to deny them that right.

Myth #3. The Social Security system returns us "our" money.

Social Security does not return us our money; it returns us other people's money. Retirees in the 1970s and 1980s got back *from* Social Security everything they contributed in a little more than a year. Including employers' contributions, and adding interest, they got back everything that was contributed (plus nonexistent interest) in two and a half years. But life expectancy was around fourteen years beyond retirement. Thus, for eleven and a half years, retirees received more than they and their employers paid into the system. The elderly mainly have had more money in the last twenty-five years because entitlement programs gave them large amounts of unearned income. Such a system could not last.

It didn't. The bargain days of Social Security are over. Someone entering the labor market in 1980 had far less lucrative expectations from Social Security. We would have done better with a private insurance system. New retirees in 2010 and later who are average wage earners will no longer receive back in benefits even the value of the Social Security taxes they and their employers paid over their work life. They will get back only 90 percent of their contributions.

As Social Security becomes less of a good deal, public support for it erodes. Our parents who retired in the 1980s got back more than 200 percent of the present value of their and their employers' tax payments. Our children retiring in 2060 will receive back in benefits only 50 percent of the value of their and their employers' taxes paid into Social Security. Our generation has been left holding the fiscal bag.

Myth #4. Social Security is fundamentally sound.

It has now become increasingly apparent that Social Security tried to do too many things for too many people. It tried to raise living standards for the elderly as well as to deal with medical bills, malnutrition, and disability — all at the same time. It simply attempted to do too much. The number of workers per retired person was eleven when Social Security started; today there are 2.9 people who work for every one who is retired, and there will soon be only two. This is a factor of the increasing life expectancy and the reduced birthrates. This system is thus highly vulnerable to economic and demographic changes.

The intermediate pessimistic projections of Social Security back in the 1980s assumed a real economic growth rate of 2.6 percent after 1995, an unemployment rate of no more than 5.5 percent beyond 1995, only a slight increase in longevity, and an increase in fertility from 1.83 to 1.96

children per mother. As we now know, all of these assumptions proved incorrect, and we are left with a system that we can't fund, that we can't count on for our own retirement, but that we must continue to fund for our parents at the expense of our children.

To the American Association of Working People, Social Security is no longer a sacred cow. We live with the reality that the ongoing erosion of Social Security's returns to its participants has affected our generation of workers. We pay the tax increases that are necessary because Social Security has been untouchable. We are the grandchildren who have been burdened by irresponsible decisions. We have inherited some $7 trillion of unfunded liabilities from entitlement programs for the elderly, and we must pay off a mortgage taken out by our parents and our grandparents.

Immigration and Integration

To make a nation truly great a handful of heroes capable of great deeds at supreme moments is not enough. Heroes are not always available and one can often do without them. But it *is* essential to have thousands of *reliable* people — honest citizens — who steadfastly place the public interest before their own.

— Pasquale Villari, 1860

Why We Closed Our Borders:
A Speech to the United Nations General Assembly by the Deputy Secretary of State July 4, 2000

Ladies and gentlemen of the General Assembly, there is an old saying in diplomacy that the speeches of most career diplomats continually careen between cliché and indiscretion. I shall try to avoid both and to speak frankly about the most explosive issue of the last twenty years: immigration.

I realize how controversial this issue has grown. I recognize that the new measure taken by the United States to limit immigration only to immediate relatives of United States citizens has been met with mixed emotions by the members of this assembly. Vice President Bill Clinton has struggled with the problem of immigration all his political career. In 1980, the establishment in his home state of Arkansas of camps for Cuban entrants — the first of the eighty camps the United States now maintains to hold apprehended illegal immigrants — caused the only defeat in his meteoric political career. No one has struggled more with this intensely human issue. But the sad fact is that we did not take controlling steps early enough — and now the only options with which we are faced are unpleasant. In public policy, the longer we ignore a problem, the fewer our options to solve it. The world's population is now more than 6 billion people. In the last twenty years, we added more people to the world than existed in 1935, and 90 percent of this growth took place on just three continents — Asia, South America, and Africa. Despite famines, which have become almost commonplace on these three continents, the United States has come to represent a smaller and smaller percentage of the world's population. Despite the geometric growth of immigration into the United States and Europe over the past two decades, the developed countries have fallen from being a third of the world's population in 1950 to a fifth today. The number of people between the ages of twenty and thirty-nine has grown by 17 million in the developed countries since 1980, while the same age group has grown by 600 million in the developing countries. Most of these young adults have their childbearing years ahead of them. We are surrounded by a sea of hungry, malnourished humanity, and we have to do some clear, hardheaded thinking.

Man has become a locust on the land. Despite our best efforts to promote family planning, despite the recent acceptance of artificial birth control methods by the Roman Catholic Church, we can confidently predict that one billion additional people will be added to the world's population in the next eleven years. We are at a critical point in our demographic history. We face the gravest threat to the future of the world since the Middle East blockade of 1988. But this is a "creeping crisis." It is difficult to arouse people to face a gradually building crisis, but our action in limiting immigration shows that we are at last facing that challenge.

As Kenneth Boulding observed, one of the dilemmas of the human condition is that our experience and knowledge are about the past, and our decisions are about the future. We have rarely succeeded in acting on even simple extrapolations; we have been "future blind," as though we could not see the road before us. It should have been painfully apparent to us, back in the 1980s, that we were going to have a massive immigration problem. In 1980, the United States accepted as many refugees and immigrants for permanent resettlement as did the rest of the world combined. We accepted 808,000 legal immigrants, and between half a million and a million illegal immigrants were also added to our population. The Cuban flotilla occurred in that year, as did a sudden spurt in illegal immigration from Haiti. These were all harbingers of a complete loss of control of our immigration system. Since 1980, immigration has accounted for 50 percent of our national growth rate.

We did not recognize, however, that our public policy must change as the world changes. One of our greatest national leaders, Abraham Lincoln, said it well: "As our case is new, so must we think anew and act anew. We must disenthrall ourselves, and then we shall save our country." America, the land of immigrants, should have seen the pressures that were forming and acted to avoid them. But we were blinded by the Statue of Liberty. Somehow, with all the surging emotions inherent in a nation of immigrants, we couldn't bring ourselves to recognize the inevitable — that the United States could not, cannot, be the home of last resort for all the dispossessed people in the world. We thought the Lady in the Harbor, a national symbol for us, wouldn't understand.

So we watched, paralyzed, as the numbers grew, and we didn't take the necessary actions to bring control. Back in 1980, one out of ten people in Los Angeles was an illegal immigrant. Of all births in Los Angeles County public hospitals in that year, 67.5 percent were to illegal immigrants. We had 6 million to 9 million illegal immigrants in the United States, and our borders were, for all practical purposes, unguarded. We had fewer people guarding our two-thousand-mile border with Mexico than guarding the 103 acres of the nation's Capitol, operating with a budget lower than that of the Baltimore Police Department.

We now understand the simple truth that a country can't have a "no border" policy any more than your home can have a "no door" policy.

I must now speak of a very delicate aspect of U.S. immigration policy. I want to quote from a recent letter to the President signed by some members of the Congressional Hispanic Caucus. "Dear President Hesperus: As elected representatives, not only of our districts but also of the Hispanic people in the United States, we applaud and encourage you in your decision to declare a moratorium on all immigration except for nuclear families of American citizens. The Hispanic American people have been sorely hurt, not only by competition in the labor force from millions of Hispanic legal and illegal immigrants, but also by the fears which have been aroused that Hispanic Americans were creating a 'Hispanic Quebec' in the American Southwest."

The fact is that immigration to the United States, for the past thirty-five years, has been dominated by members of one language group — Spanish. Since the passage of the 1965 Immigration and Nationality Act, approximately 35 percent of all legal immigrants and 60 percent of all illegal immigrants have been Spanish-speaking. This has come about largely because of geography, and through the tremendous population growth of Mexico to its present 130 million people. Yet, in our entire history, such linguistic concentration is unprecedented. Since 1980, the Hispanic population has been the fastest-growing segment of the U.S. population. We can now project, with a high degree of reliability, that by the year 2080 almost 40 percent of the population will be post-1980 immigrants and their descendants.

The 1997 riot in East Los Angeles, the rash of fire bomb-ings in Miami, in New York, and throughout the Southwest, and the three-month siege of downtown San Diego in 1998 were all led by second-generation Hispanics, the children of immigrants. In some cases, they demanded the equal use of Spanish throughout the United States. In some cases, they demanded the secession of five southwestern states as a Hispanic homeland. And in others, they were simply ex-pressing their outrage at this country. Whatever the cause of any individual outbreak of violence, we know that the last few years of civil disturbances far exceed anything that happened during the black uprisings of the 1960s. We have been experiencing a vast cultural separatism, and it has rent our country.

The Congressional Hispanic Caucus also wrote to the President: "The United States, it is clear, cannot take re-sponsibility for the unemployed and poor of Mexico." In 1980, Mexico had a labor force of 19 million people, of whom 50 percent were unemployed or seriously underem-ployed. Even then we knew that despite its oil wealth, Mex-ico would not be able to provide jobs for all its unem-ployed. But only the most hardheaded would have foreseen today's situation: a labor force of 45 million, still with 50 percent unemployment. Mexico, with only 40 percent of our population, has far more children born every year.

Our demographic nightmare has come true, not only in this country but all over the world. In the late 1970s, the International Labor Organization (ILO) projected that the developing world would have to generate 600 million to 700 million new jobs between 1980 and today, just to keep unemployment from rising. We know what happened. With hardly enough capital to house and feed their people, they have been unable to find the resources to come even close to creating the necessary number of jobs.

The United States has become an irresistible magnet. The per capita income in the United States was seven and a half times the per capita income of Mexico in 1980, and today it is ten times Mexico's per capital income. And Mexico remains one of the richer countries of the Third World.

Can a democracy maintain itself when it borders a fast-growing Third World country? Could Switzerland have maintained its democracy if it bordered India? We cannot solve our own unemployment problems, let alone those of Mexico, Haiti, Guatemala, El Salvador, and Peru.

Most people who arrive on our shores do so for the most understandable and universal of reasons — they want a better life. We cannot blame them. The blame lies not with them but with us. We should have recognized that with large-scale unemployment in the United States, with severe resource problems, with the four-year drought of the early 1990s that turned much of our western irrigated land back into desert, we could not be home to all the homeless. We should have understood that the Statute of Liberty stood for freedom, not for immigration. We should have recognized twenty years ago that we were no longer a frontier — that our melting pot, like any pot, had a bottom.

A few did. For instance, the Federation for American Immigration Reform (FAIR) was starting to raise these questions in the 1980s. England, in the spring of 1981, had what we today accept as an "immigration riot," but in what those days was thought of as a "race riot." A FAIR publication at that time stated:

The British riots have many causes, among them a high rate of unemployment and racial antagonism, but their root cause is massive immigration to England in the 1950s and 1960s. Because they were better off than they had been in their home countries, those early immigrants were able to endure their plight in the slums of English cities. But their children, the rioters of 1981, are not willing to endure the deprivations their parents did. They are not grateful to England because their parents were allowed to migrate there — with their job opportunities and horizons so limited, they cannot be expected to be grateful.

Those words apply with haunting accuracy to our present condition in the United States.

Aldous Huxley once said, "Facts do not cease to exist because they are ignored." We ignored the implications of population growth rates, although they have been apparent for the last fifty years. We didn't take seriously what Gunnar Myrdal called "the braking distance of population growth." That concept was deceptively simple: tomorrow's parents are already born; even if they have fewer children, the numbers of them are so large that a phenomenal built-in population increase is bound to occur. Thus, despite Mexico's heroic efforts at family planning since the 1988 famine, despite the drop in birthrate from five children per woman in 1930 to only two today, Mexico is still sure, barring catastrophe, to see a population of 250 million by 2030. Population growth has a momentum that, like a speeding car, takes considerable time and distance to bring under control. We ignored this concept when we could have done something about it.

This administration does not take lightly the world famine that greets the new century. I watch with horror the television news footage showing starving children the age of my grandchildren. But the numbers are too large to save. Last year's restrictions on food exports from the United States were only a recognition of the inevitable. After just a few years of low rainfall, we were growing little surplus beyond that needed to feed our own country's 300 million inhabitants.

Our first duty is to our own citizens. We are going to fulfill that duty. Under the new emergency measures passed by Congress, we have restricted immigration to the United States to immediate family members of citizens. We are tripling our border patrol and issuing new counterfeit-proof identification cards and new regulations to enable us to vigorously prosecute any employer who hires anyone illegally residing in the United States.

We have, belatedly, asked what level of immigration is in the best interest of the United States. Had we controlled immigration twenty years ago, we could have continued a generous policy indefinitely. We didn't and so we have now, of necessity, declared a moratorium on all immigration, save for those family members.

We cannot give a home to all the world's homeless. It was our mistake to try to accommodate and assimilate so many people. The Statue of Liberty stands for freedom, not for unlimited immigration. This is America's true mission: We wish to be an example of freedom and demonstrate that it is possible to have a free, decent, and caring society that can intelligently plan for its children. If we are to preserve that freedom, we must limit immigration.

Ladies and gentlemen of the General Assembly, I thank you for your attention.

The Unmelted Pot:
Report of the U.S. Civil Rights Commission
January 2000

America has had an almost mystical belief in its national ideals. It has been one of our strengths. America's image of itself was positive and optimistic, which was a dynamic of its success. America as a young and vigorous nation could solve any problem, meet any demand, execute every challenge. We absorbed an incredible number of people of diverse cultures and developed a heterogeneous but unified culture of our own.

This commission has always advocated an integrated America. We believe in racial equality and social justice. Our dream, expressed more than thirty years ago, was of an America that lived up to its promise of "equal justice under the law."

It is thus with heavy hearts and a profound sense of loss that we find that in the last ten years America has become more segregated, more divided, more Balkanized than it was thirty years ago. New racial and cultural conflicts abound, and America has not only failed to achieve equality but has reversed earlier progress. A new Jim Crow has developed in America.

We find that the southwestern United States has become a Hispanic Quebec, filled with tensions and conflict unimaginable twenty years ago. America thought it could avoid the problems that plagued other nations filled with diverse people. It worked up to a point — but it is no longer working.

Seldom has a nation had to absorb as many people as the

United States has over the last twenty-five years. Even before the revolutions in South and Central America and Mexico, the United States was absorbing large numbers of Hispanics. There were so many that integration did not operate and demands for separate linguistic and cultural treatment soon developed.

Conflict was minor at first and the early provocation was clearly not caused by Hispanics. Illegal aliens were victimized and the Ku Klux Klan took it upon itself to "enforce" new immigration laws. Violence flared in many parts of the United States. Hispanics charge "cultural genocide," while Anglos charge that bilingual education is "de-Americanizing" our nation. It is a dialogue between the blind and the deaf.

Yet the revolutions south of our border made our border unmanageable. The numbers were too large and the desperation was too great. The sanctuary movement in U.S. churches grew dramatically. Soon the distinction between legal citizen and illegal alien blurred. Blacks felt that illegal immigrants were preventing their economic advancement; conflict arose between those two groups and soon became violent.

White and black citizens, fearing economic dislocation and the rising cost of providing social services, demanded a national identification card, and the ensuing legislative battle opened wounds that still fester. Hispanic groups, understandably, felt persecuted and organized their now-famous march on Washington at which Senator Henry Cisneros made his eloquent plea for "brown power."

By the late 1980s, the Hispanic demand for the establishment of "Aztlan," a new nation, was asserted. It was argued that the United States "illegally" took the Southwest from Mexico with the 1848 Treaty of Guadalupe Hidalgo, and Mexico and Hispanic militants demanded it back. The simultaneous bombing of the immigration offices of New Mexico, Arizona, and California accented this demand. The People's Republic of Mexico pushed to "renegotiate" the treaty and for return of "Mexican property stolen from its people." Bilingual, bicultural education became less a transitional program than a demand for "cultural equality." The biggest civil rights issue today isn't the question of integration but the demand for segregation and return of land deemed "stolen."

Even the Congressional Hispanic Caucus has been pushed to the extreme. Their position on Aztlan was recently amended to say: "The U.S. government created by force an artificial boundary through the middle of Mexico in 1848 and it is arrogance to declare that those who cross this forced border are 'illegal aliens' in their own land."

We find that it is impossible to ascribe the blame for these tensions to any one event or group. Long before the assassination of the Mexican ambassador to the United States and the Los Angeles barrio riots, the breach had become irreconcilable. The United States now, tragically, has its own Quebec.

Thus we find that in America in the year 2000:

1. Our economy has not created and is not creating enough new jobs for our own citizens, let alone additional immigrants. Illegal aliens have become a large, resentful, and dangerous underclass of unskilled and untrained workers who cannot find employment.

2. We have lost control, not only over our border, but also over the size and nature of our work force, our nation's population size and policy, our linguistic heritage, and our foreign policy.

3. Not being able to control our own borders, we have been unable to control the inflow of political terrorists,

foreign agents, and everyday criminals that other countries, following Castro's example, dump on us.

4. Our energy and natural resource shortages, severe since the 1970s, have been increased and aggravated by both legal and illegal immigration.

5. Our social cohesion and political unity have been severely disrupted. Our foreign policy is now held hostage to recently arrived aliens, militantly demanding influence.

The New Segregation

The falling birthrates have been largely a Caucasian middle-class phenomenon. The birthrate of minorities has stayed even, which means that the percentage of minorities in our society is increasing. By the late 1990s, minorities of all ages accounted for 25 percent of our population — but more than 30 percent of the younger age groups.

Legal and illegal immigration is dramatically changing the face of our cities. In New York City in the 1970s, for example, the overall population declined by 10.4 percent, but the Asian population grew by 250 percent. Los Angeles now has a 60 percent Hispanic population, with 20 percent of its total population estimated to be illegal immigrants. In many parts of the United States we have lost our social and linguistic cohesion.

Meanwhile, "white flight" has unbalanced the demography of our cities. Detroit has lost 50 percent of its white population; New York City, 30 percent; Boston, 25 percent.

These figures have dramatically affected urban schools. Public schools in twenty-three of the twenty-five largest cities in the United States now have predominantly minority enrollments. The change has been fast-paced and considerable. In these school systems in 1950, one student in ten came from a minority group; by 1960 it was one in three; in 1970 it was one in two. By 1980, seven urban students out of ten were children of minorities, and by 1990 the Joint Center for Political Studies found that nine out of ten students in big-city districts were members of a minority group. In forty years the racial make-up of these urban schools has been completely reversed.

In some areas, the change has been even more startling. Los Angeles's Hispanic enrollment was 20 percent in 1968, and it had grown to 49 percent by 1982. It is now 70 percent. Similar changes took place in Dade County, Florida, and in Chicago the proportion of Hispanic students is now 20 percent, with Hispanic students replacing whites as the second-largest group of students after blacks.

Minorities made up 10 percent of the public school population in 1950, but they now make up 45 percent in many states.

Our cities have become more segregated than any area of American life — more so than in the most racist days of Jim Crow. We have a divided America, characterized by minority cities surrounded by largely white suburbs, by poverty surrounded by wealth, by the unemployed surrounded by the employed, by despair surrounded by hope. We have the dream of desegregation replaced by the reality that America has not integrated but is experiencing, at best, an armed and uneasy truce between the races. This is a prescription for disaster. Our metropolitan areas are social time bombs, powder kegs sitting in the sun.

Children Having Children:
Report of the U.S. Civil Rights Commission
June 1999

We have a crisis in black America.

Children are having children, often illegitimate ones. A large percentage of these are black children. They have produced and will continue to produce an explosion of uneducated, angry, destructive, and dangerous youth.

During the last twenty-five years, the majority of black births were illegitimate. Almost half of all black women have had their first child before their twentieth birthday. One in four black female teenagers will have an illegitimate baby by eighteen. One in eight black children is born to a girl seventeen or younger.

In addition, almost half of all black families with related children under eighteen are headed by women, and half of all black children live in female-headed households. The average income for such black households is less than one-third of the average American family income.

The sad roll call continues: 65 percent of all black pregnant teens under fifteen and half of all those aged fifteen to nineteen do not receive prenatal care in the first trimester of pregnancy. This increases birth defects, premature births, and infant mortality.

When children have children, their education is interrupted and seldom completed. They are unprepared for adulthood; their own personal potential is unfulfilled. Pregnancy is the primary reason given by girls who drop out of school. Of all mothers who had their first child before age eighteen, only half later finished high school; only 1.6 percent finished college.

A black baby has almost one in two chances of being born poor. Children born to unmarried teenage girls are four times more likely to be born poor and remain poor than children in other families.

Thirty percent of all black adolescents who gave birth became pregnant again within two years. A large number of black teenagers have a second or later child, some having four children by the time they are twenty.

Although the *rate* of birth to unmarried black teenagers decreased by 3.5 percent between 1970 and 2000, a disproportionate number of unmarried black teenagers continue to have babies. In Chicago, 91.4 percent of all births to black teenagers are illegitimate; in New York City, 89.5 percent; in Philadelphia, 92 percent; in Baltimore, 91.1 percent; in Kansas City, 89.9 percent; and in Richmond 82.7 percent.

Between 1964 and 2000 the marriage rate for black teenagers dropped by 45 percent and it will continue to decrease.

The black columnist William Raspberry pointed out in the 1980s that various welfare programs have the effect of enticing girls into adolescent motherhood because they offer free housing, medicine, food, and welfare payments to those who bear an illegitimate child.

The problem clearly transcends race. Illegitimate births have been rising for thirty years in the United States. Teenage pregnancies have quadrupled in that time.

We have made it increasingly less difficult for pregnant teenagers, both married and unmarried, to obtain medical, financial, educational, and other services. An illegitimate baby is a ticket to economic and family independence. Freedom is achieved through childbearing and subsidized by the taxpayers. Pregnant teenage children become independent, public-supported mothers and are often entitled to taxpayer-subsidized housing at the same time.

We find that these children are victims of a well-intentioned but misguided welfare system that makes it economically advantageous to have an illegitimate child. Tragically, their children often repeat the sad cycle themselves.

Crime and Terrorism

We are witnessing the erosion, perhaps the final erosion, of the idea of man as something splendid.

— Leon Kass, molecular biologist and ethicist

The Violent Decade:
Report of the President's Commission
on Violence and Terrorism
May 2000

The 1990s were clearly, by any measure, America's "violent" decade — violent in the streets, violent in the suburbs, violent within the family home, violent in the classroom. To our historic patterns of crime and violence, we have added political terrorism. America must curb this violence or we shall have a rendezvous with fascism.

Already cries are being heard for suppression of liberties — despite several dramatic Supreme Court rulings that have "untied the hands of the police." We note the prophetic words of Edward Gibbon in *The History of the Decline and Fall of the Roman Empire:* "In the end, more than they wanted freedom, they wanted security. They wanted a comfortable life, and they lost it all — security, comfort and freedom. When the Athenians finally wanted not to give to society, but for society to give to them; when the freedom they wished for most was the freedom from responsibility, then Athens ceased to be free."

Are we seeing the decline and fall of America? Opinions differ, but we believe not. America is too great, too strong, too just. Yet the trends are ominous.

The 1990s showed a continuing deterioration of city tax bases as blacks, Hispanics, and other minorities increasingly dominated the urban core and the nation increasingly divided between haves and have-nots. The erosion of the city tax base has made the expense of law enforcement more burdensome and in many cases fiscally prohibitive. Crime is growing and enforcement is shrinking.

We have seen the rise of vigilantism. Private police agencies and burglar alarm systems have been the growth industries of the 1990s. While automation in the burglar alarm industry and the property protection area has made this more efficient, the stunning increase in the need and demand has led to a new and expensive cost of doing business anywhere near American cities.

Lack of funds owing to the eroding tax base has forced police departments to concentrate on hard-core crime. Social service agencies have had to take up the slack by responding to child abuse cases, domestic incidents, and many other crime categories that used to be handled by local law enforcement. Traffic enforcement has all but ceased.

There is some good news. Law enforcement has been made considerably easier by the rise of the "electronic policeman." Automated systems now correlate large numbers of clues, information, and observations from the field and can examine thousands of crime and arrest reports, methods of operation, and seemingly unrelated incidents in order to catch criminals. There has been an explosion in technology in the last fifteen years, with new out-of-vehicle radios, in-vehicle digital terminals, and a wide variety of computer-aided communication that daily helps our law enforcement officials. Searches of records that once took weeks now take seconds, and identification of stolen vehicles and property has become much simpler. Automatic communication to local, state, and national law enforcement files is now integrated, at great convenience to the law enforcement officials.

Police chiefs and sheriffs can more intelligently and economically train and deploy personnel with modern-day technology. Video communication has definitely helped law enforcement. Computerized shooting simulators help us train officers in shoot and no-shoot situations, and mini-computers now link all U.S. law enforcement agencies, down to almost the smallest subdivision.

As more and more people have substituted credit cards for cash, we have seen a decrease in purse snatching and street robbery but a phenomenal increase in burglaries in the suburbs. Computer crimes constitute the fastest-growing sector of our crime statistics, and most of the perpetrators are college graduates.

The very controversial National Identification Act of 1991, requiring all United States citizens to carry identification, has greatly enhanced the ability of law enforcement officers to identify criminals and terrorists.

There has been a substantial increase in the conviction rate as the Supreme Court, reacting to public pressure in the 1980s and 1990s, struck down procedural impediments to law enforcement. Technological advances and the ability of witnesses to testify by video have greatly aided courts in the administration of justice.

However, the trends are mostly negative. Many communities have become walled fortresses, with private police protection, that want nothing from the urban areas they are near other than to be left alone.

In 1976, it was estimated that violent crimes were being committed at a rate of more than 12 million per year. We thought that was unacceptable, but the rates have grown substantially since then and many cities approach anarchy. The history of the 1990s, as one commentator stated so well, "was written in blood."

An MIT analyst, testifying before this commission,

warned that a child born today in America stands a greater chance of death by homicide than a soldier in World War II combat.

The only bright spot is that U.S. cities are not as besieged as most Third World cities. But this is small solace. We now have a world where two hundred cities have a population of more than one million, and urban areas of this globe have had to absorb more than one billion people over the last twenty-five years. Our cities have become unmanageable, chaotic, crime-ridden. But many Third World cities are in open revolt.

Crime and Minorities

The FBI's uniform crime report indicates that the robbery rate went up by more than 500 percent from 1945 to 1975, while the rate of all "violent crimes" (murder, rape, robbery, and aggravated assault) increased 232.8 percent between 1960 and 1983. Keep in mind also that the police and FBI estimate that only half the crimes committed are actually reported. Then, from 1975 to the year 2000, both figures, robbery and violent crimes, doubled.

These rates make the United States a violent, dangerous country compared with the rest of the civilized world. There are five times more homicides, ten times more rapes, and seventeen times more robberies in the United States than in Japan. But the violence in our cities is even more disproportionate. In the 1970s there were two hundred seventy-nine times as many robberies, fourteen times as many rapes, and twelve times as many murders in New York City as in Tokyo. Those ratios have increased even more in the last two decades.

The increase of minorities in our cities and our increasing crime rate are not unrelated. A staggering amount of our crime is committed by blacks and Hispanics living in urban areas. The magnitude of this problem demands attention. The President's Commission on the Causes of Crime and Prevention of Violence studied seventeen large American cities and found that blacks committed 72 percent of the homicides, 74 percent of the aggravated assaults, 81 percent of the unarmed robberies, and 85 percent of the armed robberies.

The executive order of 1986 forbade the correlation of race and crime statistics after that date. Yet the 1981 figures are instructive.

Crime rate statistics for 1981 show that blacks made up 12 percent of our society but were 46 percent of those arrested for violent crime, while whites made up 86 percent of the population and were 53 percent of those arrested for violent crime. Hispanics are included in the white arrest figures but, breaking those down further, we find that Hispanics constituted 6 percent of the U.S. population but made up 12 percent of the arrests for violent crime.

Of juveniles in custody in the 1980s and 1990s, 27 percent were black, whereas only 14 percent of the U.S. population aged ten to nineteen was black.

Several comprehensive studies revealed a striking resemblance between serious juvenile offenders and adult felons. There is clear evidence in these studies that a subclass of chronic, violent juvenile offenders progresses from serious juvenile to serious adult criminal careers.

Serious juvenile offenders, these studies show, like adult offenders, (1) are predominantly male; (2) are disproportionately black and Hispanic as compared to their proportion of the population; (3) are typically disadvantaged economically; (4) are likely to exhibit interpersonal difficulties and behavioral problems, both in school and on the job; and (5) often come from one-parent families or families with a high degree of conflict, instability, and inadequate supervision.

One major difference between juvenile and adult offenders, however, is the problem of juvenile "gangs." A national survey of law enforcement officials showed that the problem is disproportionately large in the big cities, but gangs are often found in cities of even less than one million population. Gang members are much more likely than other young criminals to engage in violent crime, particularly robbery, rape, assault, and weapons offenses.

It has long been claimed without supporting evidence that police overarrest minorities, but a 1983 Rand Corporation study found that police do not overarrest minorities in proportion to the kind and amount of crime they actually commit.

The black unemployment rate for the last twenty years officially averaged 12 percent, but that figure is clearly low. There is an unreported, underground unemployment among both blacks and whites who have only part-time jobs or who have quit seeking employment. The unemployment rate for minorities is probably twice the reported figure and much higher for minority youth. Black youth in Harlem have an estimated average unemployment rate of 86 percent.

Terrorism

No category of violence has risen faster than terrorism. The world's political leaders and political systems are in jeopardy. The distance between political stability and anarchy in much of the world is nine millimeters.

This commission believes that we should have seen this

problem coming. One study in the early 1980s showed that the Palestine Liberation Organization alone had claimed credit for seven terrorist actions a month, one action every four days, year-in and year-out for the previous ten years. Furthermore, each month during that time nine human beings had died; twenty were injured; and twenty-two were seized as hostages in the course of PLO terrorist activity. By 1984, the Rand Corporation found that there had been a fourfold increase in international terrorist activities since the 1972 Munich Olympics incident.

And, more alarmingly, terrorism had started to take place more frequently on U.S. soil. In 1983, a new world-wide record was set in terrorist activities. While there were "only" thirty-one terrorist incidents in the United States in 1983, seven cities accounted for most of the terrorist activity in that year: New York, Washington, Los Angeles, Miami, Chicago, San Francisco, and Detroit. Tragically, that list has grown in the 1990s.

The commission finds that terrorists are operating at both ends of the political spectrum, left and right. The Committee to End Police Oppression, the Committee to End Police Surveillance, the Front to End Oppression in El Salvador, Support for Puerto Rican Independence, Support for Brothers in Prison, all operate on the left, while the Ku Klux Klan, the Neo-Hitlerites, the Brotherhood of Aryan Nations, the National Socialist White People's Party, and the American Nazi Party operate on the right.

We find that the media, despite sincere and able attempts on the part of those in responsibility, continue to unintentionally encourage and foster the growth of terrorism. The commission, after much argument, found that this might be a problem without a solution. It is interesting to note that in 356 B.C., a man named Herostratos burned down the famous temple of Diana at Ephesus, thus destroying one of the seven wonders of the world. When he was caught, he admitted that he had burned the magnificent temple to gain recognition. He explained that he had no talents to make him famous so he was determined to become infamous.

The government of Ephesus, recognizing the dilemma that exists to this day, decided that no history books or writings would mention the criminal's name. But, alas, Herostratos's name has survived through the centuries. He is perhaps the godfather of today's terrorists, for it is the same motivation, the media wildfire that results from violent acts, that remains a similar but greatly expanded problem. Today's afternoon terrorist attack in Europe reaches the morning news in the United States. Tragically, the drama of many of these terrorist activities has allowed television to approach fictional literature in the magnitude and horror of the events that are covered.

Terrorism is as old as history. But the high stakes today, and the many vulnerabilities of society, make the terrorist a special concern. With instant communications and all sorts of electronic media available, terrorists can demand and succeed in drawing immediate attention; but even more, they have the potential of bringing this society to a standstill. The stakes are the very survival of our system.

This commission specifically finds:

1. We live in a world where limited conventional war, classic guerrilla warfare, and international terrorism coexist, with some governments and some subnational causes using all of them interchangeably, sequentially, and often simultaneously.
2. The 1990s saw a much higher order of violence of all types, including an explosion of extortion attempts by criminals, by terrorists, by mental patients, by adolescents. These included false threats on a U.S. city to

poison the water supply and to detonate a nuclear de-
vice. Actual events included the destruction of hotels,
the bombing of mass transit systems, and numerous
kidnappings of public and private officials.

3. A number of well-meaning but tragically mistaken
groups in the United States actually encourage terrorism. The phrase that is often heard out of the mouths
of these deluded people — "One man's terrorist is another man's freedom fighter" — has partly masked the
real truth to America: that, for the first time in our
history, the very existence of our democratic institutions is threatened by a small group of people who
obey no rules. We find that one democracy's terrorist
is another democracy's terrorist. Terrorism is a viola-
tion of the fundamental rights of democratic citizens.

4. Only a handful of countries accounts for three-quarters of all terrorist activities. Nearly half of all the
world's terrorism targets are in the United States,
Great Britain, Germany, France, and Israel.

5. There has been a large and very worrisome acquisition
by political extremists of sophisticated weapons, including missile launchers and a large amount of explosives. Mining the seas has become a new tool of international terrorism.

6. As we all know from the tragic events of the past four
decades, political assassination is a fact of life. The
self-discipline of terrorists is starting to disappear, and
we are now witnessing a rise in the number of indiscriminate murders.

7. Federal regulations in the United States make the purchase of explosives laughably easy. Prospective buyers
must do little more than fill out a one-page form,
swearing that they are not felons, mental defectives, or
drug users, and that they plan to use the explosives

legally. The regulations governing this have no limits on the amount of explosives any buyer can obtain, nor is there any waiting period as there is with the purchase of firearms, nor is there any cumulative total at which purchases over time must be cut off. Terrorists as well as technicians, marauders as well as miners, can pay their money and walk out the door carrying explosives. In many places, it is easier to purchase a case of dynamite than a gun.

8. It is becoming increasingly hard to separate "freedom fighters" and "national liberation movements" from the old-fashioned terrorists. The Soviet Union, while claiming to support only national liberation movements, in fact since the foundation of the Terror International in 1966, has been spiritually, monetarily, or physically behind a large number of the terrorist groups. But it would be a serious mistake to think that all terrorist movements are sponsored by the Soviet Union. They are not. Colonel Muammar el-Qaddafi's argument, pressed now for thirty years as a justification for his violence, is "Why should we Muslims listen to Western laws written by Christians and Jews five hundred years ago? We live by the Koran."

9. The sources of terrorism are deep-rooted: in suspicion, revenge, hatred — emotional reasons that are not necessarily amenable to rational argument and debate. Rational concessions will not influence fanaticism's ideological objectives.

10. Last, but first among our concerns, is nuclear terrorism. We now know that nuclear weapons have fallen into the hands of terrorist groups, religious fanatics, and Third World dictators. Pakistan has developed an "Islamic bomb" and Argentina has a "Latin bomb." In the 1980s, the United States put its commercial inter-

ests ahead of its security interests and made available
the plutonium and technology to build these devices.
We now live in a world where the genie is truly out of
the bottle and at the command of unstable, irrational
fanatics, both political and religious. Like the pistol
shot at Sarajevo that triggered the start of World War
I, a terrorist act could begin a chain reaction engulfing
the world in the final world war.

Memorandum

To: The President
From: The Director of the Bureau of Prisons
Re: Prisonia
Date: January 20, 2001

Some twenty years ago, a former warden, William Nagel,
warned that the United States was heading toward having
a criminal population that would be equivalent in size to
our sixth largest city. He named his mythical city Prisonia.
He pointed out that in 1979 Prisonia was a city of slightly
under 500,000, the total of all prisoners in American prisons and jails, and that it was a city larger than Denver and
had a larger population than three of our states. He
warned, "Watch out, New Orleans, Boston, Cleveland, and
San Francisco. Prisonia will be bigger than any of you."

Madam President, the fearful reality is that in the last
decade Prisonia became our fifth largest city, larger than
Detroit, and the situation gets worse year by year.

The population of Prisonia is disproportionately young,
poor, black, Hispanic, and male — with a nightmarish

array of social pathologies, including drug abuse, alcoholism, sexual deviation, and mental illness. It is full of fear and rage and it has resisted any attempts at amelioration.

One of the problems of our society, Madam President, is that crime does seem to pay! There are benefits to crime for poor, young, unemployed urban males. If they choose to get a regular job, they face a staggering uphill battle to find a decent one. Even if they land a job — and chances are no more than one in three — it is likely to be a dead-end job with no future.

The rewards of a life of crime are money, excitement, and, in a strange way, an elevation in status among one's peers. In the subculture of the inner city, the choice looks much more tempting than it does to middle-class Americans. The rewards seem to outweigh the relatively small possibility that the criminal will go to prison.

What happens if we incarcerate more people — let's say double the size of Prisonia? What do we achieve? Studies back in the 1980s showed that a 264 percent increase in prison population would be necessary to reduce serious street crime in New York State by just 10 percent. In Ohio, a study suggested that sending all felony offenders to prison for five years would reduce violent crime by only 4 percent. If we chose that alternative, we would make Prisonia one of our largest cities.

And, even if we were to adopt that solution, we still would have the same social pathology producing a new generation of criminals every year. To expand Prisonia at a cost of $60,000 per person incarcerated is a burden that the taxpayers simply cannot bear. Yet the crime rate continues to rise unabated and unfortunately all America is now in the front lines on the war on crime.

We are thus caught in a dilemma: a rising tide of crime and violence and not enough resources to lock up all those who deserve to be behind bars.

Breakdown

The purpose of long-range forecasts generally is not just to satisfy mankind's persistent curiosity about its future destiny but . . . to inform decision makers in both public and private sectors . . . of potential future dangers that must be avoided and of potential future opportunities that must be seized.

— Olaf Helmer, "Planting Seeds for the Future"

The future ain't what it used to be.

— Arthur C. Clarke, *The Adventure of Tomorrow*

The Death of the American City: Special Report from the Department of Housing and Urban Development October 1, 2000

This department must now accept the fact that the large American cities (New York, Los Angeles, Chicago, Philadelphia, Detroit, Houston, Baltimore, Dallas, and Cleveland) have virtually ceased to function as national centers, and that nearly forty of our midsized cities are in a similar process of degeneration. The historic role of the metropolis as a center of economic activity, production, cultural excellence, and social change has disappeared. The most pessimistic predictions of the urbanologists of the 1970s have proved to be only too true. The tragedy they foresaw has happened.

The evident decay of the cities in the late 1970s — whose dramatic high point was the near-bankruptcy of New York City — was followed, of course, by an era of renewed hope through most of the 1980s. Many of the older, declining neighborhoods underwent renovation and gentrification, as a result of the back-to-the city movement of young and relatively affluent professionals. Fashionable new retail-shop areas were created in what had been depressed portside sections of Baltimore, Boston, New York, San Francisco, and elsewhere. It was a decade of hope for an urban renascence.

Unfortunately, as we have observed through the 1990s,

the forces of destruction and decay have gradually won the battle for the cities. As the new, affluent class restored Back Bay or Society Hill, the ghetto and slum areas of cities grew more formidable and more lawless. Middle-class ethnic neighborhoods — in a movement that began in the 1960s — gradually gravitated toward suburban areas. Middle-class and upwardly mobile black families moved from the Harlems and the Chicago South Sides to their own suburbs. The slums and ghettos increasingly became enclaves inhabited by no one but the desperately poor and the criminal class. Thus, American cities became dangerously polarized. With the middle classes evicted, they ended, in the 1990s, as different versions of Beirut — partitioned between a fortified enclave of the rich and a battlefield ruled by predators and partially inhabited by the captive poor.

Today, the media are full of vivid images attesting to the fate of the cities. We now realize that the South Bronxes and Bedford-Stuyvesants of the 1980s were visions of the future. The typical inner city of the year 2000 is a vast area of dilapidated brick and cement. It is thinly populated (though only in comparison with the former overcrowding) and is nearly 100 percent black, Hispanic, or Southeast Asian. There are no longer banks, hospitals, retail stores, garages, or small industries of any kind. Food and other necessities can be bought in neighborhood street markets, but the supply is unreliable and the prices are, for the poor, exorbitant. Police and fire protection are minimal as a result of the unacceptable casualties suffered in the past ten years. Few blocks, if any, retain electricity, gas, water, or telephone services.

There is no government left — these slums are Balkanized. Except for the no man's lands, each district is ruled by one gang. Crime is the major activity and the drug trade is the major commerce. There are no courts, no tax collection, no census, no postal service, and very little news coverage. This report is necessary, in fact, not because these conditions are unknown but because the rest of America has largely written off the cities as desert areas to be ignored.

Within most large cities there have survived what we have previously described as fortress cities of the rich — the northern strip of lakeshore in Chicago, midtown Manhattan and the east and west borders of Central Park, for example. In a much reduced way, they perform most of the traditional functions of the former metropolis. They are centers of banking and finance, communications, government and legal systems, and industry headquarters of various kinds. Wall Street, LaSalle Street, and the Civic Center still carry on, even though this department believes that all such fortresses are doomed within the next decade or two.

The high-income professionals and specialists who remain are like garrisons in hostile lands. The neo-castle movement in city architecture, which began in the 1960s, is now universal. There are no windows in the lower stories of residential buildings. Store display windows are a thing of the past. Security guards — human, canine, and electronic — are present at every entrance of a building. Everyone is used to giving voiceprint and fingerprint identification. Metal-detector gates are ubiquitous in all public buildings. No office, apartment, bank, or shop is without a sophisticated alarm system. Most fortress-city dwellers have permits to carry the new, highly effective stun-gun pistols. The computerized police system has at its disposal every form of equipment from armored cars to helicopter gunships.

The midtwentieth-century city, whatever its drawbacks, now looks like Happy Valley in comparison with the new reality. Except for police cars and bulletproof vehicles of the very rich, streets are deserted. The former subway systems — or new ones — are the transportation arteries for the privileged. They are among the most carefully monitored areas of the cities.

Most children in this new society have seen their cities from the twentieth story. They have never played in a park, walked down a street, or sat on a beach — except on vacation in Geneva, Stockholm, or St. Tropez.

The fortress cities are, of course, quite as doomed as the slum cities. They have served a transitional function as service and communications centers, but that function is now being taken over by the vast electronic communications networks that link all parts of the continent. Within the near future, for instance, "Wall Street" will become a large computer center thirty miles north of Albany and all transactions will be electronic.

Urban rot has made no geographical distinctions. While the rustbelt cities have had their centers of despair in black ghettos, sunbelt cities have watched themselves being ringed by the shacks of barrio towns crowded with illegal immigrants. Violent-crime-rate records that used to be held by Chicago or Detroit are now outdone in Houston or Los Angeles.

At the same time, the former suburbs of cities, the greenbelt sanctuaries for the white flight that began in the 1960s, have now inherited all the inner-city problems of the 1960s, '70s, and '80s. Urban blight, crime, drugs, racial conflicts, and congestion have spread to the Shady Hills and the Lake Bluffs that used to lie at the peaceful end of the commuter line. Most of these, too, seem to be doomed.

It is the belief of this department that the former sites of most large American cities must be condemned as living areas and effectively sanitized. Within the next six months, a detailed plan for this action will be offered to the President by the Secretary.

This plan will call for condemnation of large urban areas. These would be ceded to the federal government by the states and then placed under martial law. The populace would be cleared and processed — the victimized poor assigned housing and job opportunities in other parts of the country, known criminals sent to prison camps, and drug addicts put in rehabilitation centers.

Each city site would then be redeveloped according to its best potential use. Chicago, for instance, might have key buildings and its university campuses preserved in order to create a twenty-first-century-style city of universities and small, high-tech production areas separated by parklands and greenbelts. Cleveland, it is possible, might undergo years of salvaging for all usable materials and then be bulldozed and its site finally reforested as a national park.

We believe that America's experiment with huge cities has come to a natural end. We further believe that half-ruined remains of these areas are an evident danger to the health of the nation as a whole. It is, therefore, our recommendation that the old, no-longer-viable cities of America be eliminated.

Report from the Commissioner of the Internal Revenue Service December 2000

Madam President, it is clear that we have a serious breakdown in the self-assessment tax system that has worked so well for this country for almost a hundred years. It can be seen both in the growth of the underground economy and in the dramatic rise in the cost of maintaining the income tax enforcement system.

This breakdown is a trend. It became evident in 1984, when it was estimated that $100 billion of income escaped taxation. This happened in a wide variety of ways: one cause was an increase in the use of barter; another derived from the duplicity of people who kept two sets of books. The underground economy was estimated in 1984 to be 25 percent of the total economy, and it has now grown to 50 percent, or $300 billion in current dollars.

The cost of enforcing compliance has grown dramatically, and tax evasion has become a new form of civil disobedience. Basically honest citizens, who wouldn't think of jaywalking, now think of themselves as victims of a tax structure in which they have no confidence. Oliver Wendell Holmes, Jr., said, "Taxes are what we pay for civilized society." But a common current attitude is that tax dollars aren't buying much of that. They feel cheated and foolish in view of the wide publicity given to certain high-income corporations and individuals who take advantage of loopholes and pay no taxes. The underground economy and tax evasion have become the poor man's tax shelter. Stories of people making a million dollars a month but paying no income tax and reports that 50 percent of America's large corporations pay no corporate income tax have so under-cut the credibility of the tax system that tax cheating has become a national ethic. We now approach Italy and France in the cynicism and dishonesty with which our citizens relate to the tax system.

Taxes are traditionally judged according to three public finance criteria: simplicity, equity, and efficiency. A simple tax is one that is easy to comply with and to administer. An equitable tax is one that treats people in equal economic circumstances similarly (horizontal equity) and people in different economic circumstances differently (vertical equity, or progressivity). An efficient tax is one that does not distort economic decisions, especially those involving work savings in an allocation of capital.

The U.S. income tax system is none of the above. Taxpayers spent 600 million hours in 1999 filling out tax forms, and more than 60 percent of all taxpayers had to resort to professional help from one of 120,000 tax lawyers and accountants in the country. In 1982, taxpayers spent 300 million hours filling out tax forms and 40 percent of them had to resort to professional help from 80,000 tax lawyers and accountants. The irony is that if one pays any substantial taxes, it is felt that one does not have a good enough tax counsel. Tax shelters, which were a $19 billion industry in 1982, have more than tripled in the last eighteen years.

Critics charge that there is little or no equity in the U.S. income tax system. An income tax system that forgoes $600 billion in tax expenditure (as compared with $330 billion in 1983), must have relatively high marginal rates to ensure adequate revenue intake. These high marginal rates in turn encourage taxpayers either to fail to report their income or to shift their behavior to qualify for a preference.

Finally, there is little efficiency in the current income tax system. It distorts economic decisions in a number of ways. High marginal rates penalize work and discourage the taxpayers who can't find shelters, or who choose not to cheat, from earning the most money possible. The failure to tax in-kind income distorts compensation figures, because employers are encouraged to give in-kind benefits instead of wages. In addition, the varying effect of tax rates on different classes of investments is a national nightmare.

In a democracy, the government has to rely on the patriotism and honesty of its citizens as taxpayers. One can never hire enough Internal Revenue Service agents to ensure that almost all of the tax gets collected. A breakdown in the confidence that people have in their tax system causes a breakdown in collectability and enforceability.

Just for the simple purposes of collecting the revenue to run the government and meet the problems that face this administration, we have to redefine a good tax in terms other than simplicity, equity, and efficiency. I would suggest to you in desperation that the overriding consideration in our tax efforts must be a tax that is collectable by means other than with the cooperation of citizens.

One historian contemporary to the fall of Rome described the relationship of tax evasion to Rome's decline: "Taxation, however harsh and brutal, would still be less severe and brutal if all shared equally in the common lot. But the situation is made more shameful and disastrous by the fact all do not bear the burden together. The tributes due from the rich are extorted from the poor."

Memorandum

To: The President
From: The Attorney General
Re: Constitutional Time Bombs
Date: January 20, 2001

Madam President, the U.S. Constitution contains two serious flaws. The Electoral College is the first time bomb ticking away in our Constitution, just waiting for the right circumstances to go off. As you know, the election of 1992 almost set off this time bomb, and it would seem that there are few worse threats to the structure of our nation than Article II of the U.S. Constitution. It is ironic, with all of the problems facing your administration, that the marvelous institution that is the United States could ultimately dissolve and be reduced to chaos by the very Constitution that is its foundation. Arnold Toynbee observed, "The same elements that build up an institution eventually lead to its downfall." The sad fact of this particular problem is that it is so unnecessary, as a simple constitutional amendment could cure it in a short period of time.

The intent of the framers of the Constitution in adopting the Electoral College was to take into account the views of its citizens, but not to be bound by them. This is little recognized, and like the fact that each slave was counted as only three-fifths of a person for purposes of the census, it is an anachronism in our Constitution. Changes in literacy and communication have rendered this provision obsolete for several reasons.

The first and most important problem with the Electoral College is that the popular vote winner can lose the election unless he also has a majority of electoral votes. It is theoretically possible for a candidate to have one-fourth of the total popular vote and still be elected President of the United States if he carries the eleven largest states and one other state. Thus it is hypothetically possible for a U.S. President to lose the popular vote and lose thirty-eight states and still win the election.

This disproportion between electoral and popular votes could undercut our entire system. Though it was much commented upon in the election of 1968, and again in the election of 1992, it would be a very volatile situation to have a majority winner of votes in the United States lose the presidency because of such an outmoded institution as the Electoral College.

A second defect is the process that is provided for if no candidate has a majority of electoral votes. The Constitution requires that the House of Representatives select the President from the top three candidates in terms of votes cast and that the Senate select the Vice President from the two top candidates. The danger of this process is that House members *could* cast their votes against the candidate who carried their district or state. If the House follows party lines, and the House majority belongs to the party that lost the popular vote, then that party would win the presidency. In addition, this is a one-vote-per-state system that makes the role of the third-party candidates much more important. Also it is very possible that the House and the Senate could select a split ticket.

A third defect in the system is the unpredictability of the pledge electors, inasmuch as the Constitution does not require them to vote for their party's candidate. Each state has control over the manner in which the electors are chosen. Once selected, and generally this is now done by popular vote, they do not have to follow the election results.

They can be unfaithful to their states and thus, in another way, cause a constitutional crisis.

Thus the Electoral College has the potential to jeopardize the legitimacy of our system. It can award the office to the popular-vote loser; it can tie up the process in the House of Representatives; and it also could result in an independent candidate gathering enough votes from a major-party candidate to elect the other major-party candidate to the presidency. This was potentially possible in 1968 with George Wallace and in 1976 with Eugene McCarthy.

There are a number of other subtleties involved in this process, but the major outline of the problem is contained above. It must be noted, however, that if the process goes into the House of Representatives and if the House of Representatives has not elected a President by inauguration day, then the Vice President–elect acts as the President until the House reaches a decision. There are too many scenarios that could cause serious disruption to take the risk of retaining this anachronism. I urge you to take the lead in seeking its repeal.

The second constitutional time bomb is Article V, setting forth how the U.S. Constitution may be amended. One of those amendment methods is that Congress, "on the Application of the Legislatures of two thirds of the several States, shall call a Convention for proposing Amendments . . ." This provision has never been utilized, but we have come close. Both the drive to modify the Supreme Court's one-person, one-vote ruling and the balanced budget amendment received applications from thirty-two state legislatures. Direct election of senators also missed by one state. That, Madam President, is too perilously close to disaster.

The disaster is that this method of amending the Constitution calls for a national constitutional convention and no one knows what a new constitutional convention might do to the basic governmental structure of this country.

The present U.S. Constitution is the product of a convention that was expressly convened "for the sole and express purpose of revising the Articles of Confederation." The first thing that 1787 convention did was to violate its specific congressional instructions; it scrapped the Articles of Confederation totally and replaced them with a new governmental structure. The precedent is thus there for a "runaway" constitutional convention that could potentially radically change our governmental structure. It could amend or delete the Bill of Rights. It would place on the table our entire constitutional structure.

Despite the urging of the American Bar Association and numerous constitutional scholars, Congress has never passed legislation limiting or defining the procedures for implementing Article V. Thus the method of selecting delegates, the subject matters to be considered, the composition and financing of such a convention, and many other important questions are unresolved. The action of thirty-four states is thus likely to commence a constitutional crisis.

PAC Man:
Report of the U.S. Election Commission
April 2000

Our politicians in the United States are for sale. Our political contests are no longer a search for truth but a search for funds. Political Action Committees (PACs) contribute half the money to elect our congressmen (up from one in three dollars in 1984). Public policy winners are not those with the best argument but those with the biggest bank account. Our Congress is filled with million-dollar PAC men and women.

We remind America of the poet who warned, "Whose bread I eat, his song I sing." There is precious little difference between a large campaign contribution and a bribe.

The system clearly favors incumbents. They receive six times more PAC funds than do their challengers (up from four times in 1984) and more than half the members of Congress receive at least half their funds from PACs. The amount of money spent by PACs roughly doubled *every* election between 1974 and 1990, and has doubled every two elections since then.

America is for sale to the highest bidder.

Poisoning America:
National Academy of Sciences Report
May 2000

America, as did the Romans, has poisoned itself. In Rome people drank wine from lead-lined storage jugs because they knew nothing about metal poisoning. In America we knew the hazards full well, but ignored them. We not only ignored the problem, but even after numerous warnings, we effected only a tepid, inadequate response. The result is a poisoned nation.

The inadequate disposal of toxic and hazardous wastes and their contamination of the groundwater has become the premier environmental and public health problem facing the United States in the year 2000. They are adding a significant disease burden to the United States. Indiscriminate dumping of toxic and hazardous waste is a public health time bomb, the full extent of which we are only trying to begin to understand. We have thoughtlessly contaminated two of our most valuable and irreplaceable natural resources, our land and our water.

Back in 1982, Senator Albert Gore warned, "Hazardous waste may be the single most significant health issue of the decade. Many Americans are justly concerned about the problems of disposing of our nuclear wastes. Yet total nuclear wastes produced to date are estimated to be under a hundred million pounds. By contrast, ninety-two billion pounds of nonnuclear waste are generated each and every year and these wastes are disposed of cavalierly."

In the year 2000 there are 84 million pounds of spent fuel, one billion pounds of defense nuclear waste, and 39 billion pounds of uranium mill tailings in storage and disposal facilities.

At the end of World War II, the United States produced a total of one billion pounds of hazardous wastes per year. The rate of production of such wastes has increased about 10 percent per year. The Environmental Protection Agency now estimates that around one trillion pounds of nonnuclear hazardous waste material are generated annually, about 3900 pounds of hazardous waste for every inhabitant of the United States, up from 80 billion pounds, or 350 pounds per person, in 1984. Even with the Resource Conservation and Recovery Act, only 30 percent of the waste is being disposed of properly.

In disposing of toxic wastes, we are finding that there is no such thing as a safe landfill. They all leave a deadly legacy. Toxic waste landfills always present society with unpleasant surprises. They leak their poisons around the modern technologies. The waste from the carelessly and negligently constructed Love Canal site was put in modern and carefully constructed toxic waste landfills. They still leaked. Barrels disintegrate, landfill liners rot, water tables change, and the toxic wastes inevitably end up contaminating our water supplies.

Instead of recognizing the need to ultimately recycle or incinerate the wastes, we tried to bury them "out of sight." But they came back to haunt us.

More than 5 million chemicals have been described in the chemical literature. Of course, most are not hazardous to humans; but identifying those that harm or have a potential for harm has occupied toxicologists for decades and we still have inadequate answers.

Pesticides and drugs have undergone the most extensive testing and yet we have health hazard assessments for only 10 percent of the pesticides and 18 percent of the drugs.

Our ignorance continues to be gargantuan. We still have inadequate or unavailable data for 80 percent of the chemicals used in America, and our information is inadequate for most of the other 20 percent. Yet a thousand new chemicals are added to American commerce each year.

Back in 1984, we found that, of the 48,523 chemicals in active commerce, no toxicity information was available for 79 percent of them. That ratio of ignorance continued to hold through the 1990s.

There has been an explosive growth of petroleum-based organic chemistry in making many useful products — synthetic fibers, pesticides, wood preservatives, plastics, drugs, paints, and solvents.

The major categories of hazardous waste are:

1. Radioactive materials.
2. Heavy metals — lead, arsenic, zinc, cadmium, copper, and mercury.
3. Asbestos.
4. Acids and base acids.
5. Synthetic organic chemicals.

A 1984 congressional survey of the nation's fifty-three largest chemical manufacturers showed that even the largest industries know very little about the fate of the waste oil and sludge they generate. About 40 percent of the sixteen hundred facilities surveyed reported they had no idea where their wastes ended up.

Congress's Office of Technology Assessment estimated that in 1985 it would cost up to $100 billion over fifty years to clean up the ten thousand sites where hazardous wastes have been dumped. In the year 2000 we have really hardly begun, and the cost has skyrocketed.

A 1984 survey by the National Governors' Association identified more than fourteen hundred areas in the United

States that were closed or had their use restricted because of toxic contamination. Most are still with us.

In the year 2000 the result of this public policy myopia is staggering. The categories of impact themselves tell the sad story: human health, habitat destruction, contamination of groundwater and water supply, contamination of topsoil, destruction of fish and livestock.

Groundwater

Contamination of our nation's groundwater was the environmental horror story of the 1990s. It will continue to plague us in the future.

Groundwater accounts for 50 percent of the nation's public water supply. Several major cities, such as Memphis and Miami, are entirely dependent on groundwater, and the U.S. Geological Survey estimates that 95 percent of all rural Americans obtain their drinking water from wells. In over thirty states, more than a third of the population consuming public water supplies uses groundwater exclusively. Americans annually withdraw 30 trillion gallons of water from the ground, and the use is increasing at 25 percent per decade.

There are 30,000 to 50,000 surface impoundments in the United States that contain liquid hazardous wastes, which are unlined, unmonitored, and above drinking water supplies.

The House Committee on Energy and Commerce's Subcommittee on Oversight and Investigations reported in September 1979: "It must also be said that industry has shown laxity, not infrequently to the point of criminal negligence, in soiling the land and adulterating the waters with its toxins. And it cannot be denied that Congress has shown lethargy in legislating controls and appropriating funds for their enforcement. As a result, even an extraordinary effort, commenced immediately, cannot achieve protection for the American public for years to come."

The examples are clear and dramatic.

The riverbed of the Hudson River in New York State is contaminated with cancer-causing PCBs as a result of past negligent disposal; in the so-called Valley of the Drums, near Louisville, Kentucky, between 17,000 and 100,000 drums of toxic waste were dumped illegally to spill their dangerous contents into a local river; in Byron, Illinois, 1500 containers of hazardous waste were buried and contaminated groundwater with cyanide, arsenic, chromium, and other toxic compounds; in Saltsville, Virginia, an industrial plant dating back to 1895 left deposits of mercury-contaminated soil that contaminated the Holsten River; in Pichens, South Carolina, a manufacturer dumped dozens of capacitors and transformers leaking PCBs into the local watershed and seriously contaminated local drinking water. The public health cost of these kinds of actions is incalculable.

In some cases, the government itself is to blame:

At the Rocky Mountain Arsenal outside Denver, Colorado, the U.S. Army dumped 2 billion gallons of chemical warfare and pesticide residues, causing thirty square miles of groundwater to become contaminated.

Near Golden, Colorado, at a U.S. government defense facility, plutonium-contaminated wastes have been wind-blown across many acres of land near residential areas. Disregarding the 49,000-year half-life of plutonium, a public park and drinking water reservoir were built on this land.

As a result of uranium procurement for the nuclear weapons program, the U.S. government has abandoned 11 million tons of radioactive uranium mill tailings at nine locations in Colorado, most of which are in the flood plains of major rivers and near populated areas.

Americans generally believe their drinking water to be safe. However, an analysis of the drinking water in a number of major metropolitan areas has disclosed the presence of several hundred synthetic organic chemicals. Cincinnati alone found seven hundred synthetic organic chemicals in its drinking water.

We did not know the long-term effects of these low levels of exposure to chemicals, but we conducted an experiment on 240 million Americans to find out. Will we ever know the true cost of our chemical abuse?

While over 48,000 chemicals are in common commercial use, the federal government has established standards for only 18 chemicals in drinking water.

Because of the twenty- to forty-year latency period of many of these chemicals, we are just beginning to reap the consequences of decades of ignorance and misuse.

Until 1976, there was no federal requirement that most chemicals be tested prior to use. Even since this time, the government has been nearly totally dependent upon industrys' own testing of their chemicals.

Not only do these chemicals cause cancer, liver and kidney damage, and other diseases; some cause deformities in future generations.

In some cases our good intentions have resulted in unforeseen results. The use of chlorine for disinfecting water also changes some harmless contaminates in the water into potentially cancer-causing chemicals.

The health effects of this environmental irresponsibility, while vast, can be summed up, with apologies to John F. Kennedy, by these words: "Ask not what your country can do *for* you; ask what it is doing *to* you."

Society, perhaps without even knowing it, has chosen to pay the debilitating costs of needless medical care rather than pay for the costs of proper waste disposal. Few Americans stopped to consider the toxic legacy that is being left to future generations. We may never be able to clean it all up.

We rushed ahead in ignorance, thinking we could "throw away" toxic and hazardous wastes. We thought the earth and the water would hide our negligence. The sad fact is that we left this problem, like so many others, to our children — and the economic and health costs will burden them for decades to come.

Education

Our nation is at risk. Our once unchallenged pre-eminence in commerce, industry, science and technological innovation is being overtaken by competitors throughout the world . . . The educational foundations of our society are presently being eroded by a rising tide of mediocrity that threatens our very future as a nation and a people. What was unimaginable a generation ago has begun to occur — others are matching and surpassing our educational attainments.

If an unfriendly foreign power had attempted to impose on America the mediocre educational performance that exists today, we might well have viewed it as an act of war . . . We have, in effect, been committing an act of unthinking, unilateral educational disarmament.

— from the National Commission on Excellence in Education's "A Nation at Risk" (1983)

Report Card on American Education from the Secretary of Education
June 2000

The year 2000 finds America with a second-rate educational system turning out second-rate students. The educational decline in our nation is truly "the new American tragedy."

"Our progress as a nation," said John F. Kennedy, "can be no swifter than our progress in education . . . The human mind is our fundamental resource."

In today's world, more than any other time in the past, a child without an education is a child without a future. The future belongs to those with the skills, training, and education to take advantage of the fast-moving economies within a fast-moving world. A child without an adequate education will be a displaced person in a world that is moving with increased velocity.

Though the United States has stabilized the drop in Scholastic Aptitude Test scores (between 1963 and 1980, verbal scores fell fifty points, math scores forty points), it is still not meeting its own standards of forty years ago — nor is it meeting the international competition.

Twenty percent of American adults are functionally illiterate. A fifth of the existing work force is thus unable to read simple instructions. There are more adult illiterates in the United States than students in both public and private secondary schools. Fifty percent of all urban students are estimated to have serious reading problems. Twenty-five percent of all college mathematics courses are remedial, and Americans are falling further and further behind when compared with students of other nations.

Education thus relates to our national wealth and productivity. America has structural unemployment and a large number of dislocated workers. Many of these disadvantaged workers not only lack job-specific training but, more important, don't have the basic skills prerequisite to being trainable and employable. One-third of our dislocated workers lack a high school diploma and another third have diplomas but are still functionally illiterate.

Many of our urban schools are entirely black. In these areas, public schools are for disadvantaged, low-income, poverty-level minority students. Most of these students are from single-parent families.

Studies show that children from intact middle-class white families perform far better than children from poor, single-parent, black, and Hispanic homes. The link between background and achievement has been demonstrated. Eighty percent of high school students surveyed who got A's lived with two parents, while only eleven percent of the A students lived with one parent.

America faces the choice of either lowering its standard of living or increasing its educational capabilities. Our economic future depends upon our national ability to excel in a variety of technologies, and the underlying ability to achieve this depends upon our education. The future of a nation and its productivity depends on the knowledge and skill of its workers. No other resource even approaches an educated citizenry as our most valuable one. Our ability to have a competitive advantage in a new emerging world economy and our ability to achieve equal economic opportunity for all are directly correlated with our ability to provide education for all persons. Simply stated, if we don't re-establish our excellence in education, our children will end up working for the Japanese.

There has been a decline in the quality not only of our students but of our teachers. Academic standards for those entering teacher training have become less stringent. Those who graduate and go into education have lower scores than their counterparts twenty years ago. There has been a steady erosion in the type of academic credentials held by teachers who remain in the system.

At the same time, there has been a dramatic rise in violence in our schools. Each month three and a half million students are victims of robbery or theft, more than a quarter of a million students suffer physical attacks, ten thousand teachers are robbed, one hundred twenty-five thousand teachers are threatened with physical harm, and at least a thousand teachers are assaulted so severely that they require medical care.

We are losing some of our best teachers to what can only be described as "educational battle fatigue."

A second-rate education is rapidly making America a second-rate power intellectually. What inevitably follows is that we become a second-rate economic and political power in the world. What our children don't know can destroy America.

The Dark Ages of Higher Education

During the last twenty years, higher education enrollments have fallen dramatically, funds going into higher education have declined precipitously, and it is clear that the system is drastically changed from what it was in 1980. In many ways we have entered a new dark age of higher education.

Enrollments have fallen because the traditional college-age generation of eighteen- to twenty-one-year-olds has been affected by a number of economic and demographic trends. One is that a labor market glut is driving down the salaries of college graduates, making a college degree a less attractive credential. It is no longer a ticket into the middle class. There are many fewer people in the college-age group, and other public services have demanded so much of the federal budget that the result has been to reduce the resources available to higher education. Thus, there has been a dramatic decline in enrollments (figures are some 40 percent lower this year than in 1980) and far less funds have been available. Universities and colleges that in the past had to deal with fast growth now must manage decline.

Colleges and universities are competing for scarce students in a variety of cannibalistic ways — for example, by offering easy courses, grade inflation, and phony academic credits. Little is asked, little is expected. Colleges recruit students who are gravely lacking in qualifications for higher education. Public confidence in higher education is at a low ebb.

Institutions offer courses to satisfy every possible desire. Endless shifts in student taste have resulted in loss of quality controls and reduction in the number of required courses. College curricula have become smorgasbords designed to appeal to students, not to educate them. The percentage of "A" grades has more than doubled in the last ten years.

Students, recognizing that they are very much in demand, have welcomed these lowered standards and have gravitated to the entertaining and unchallenging courses and to the professors who teach without much rigor. Standards on course time, content, and achievement have fallen dramatically. Gone is any quality control. Colleges accept this state of affairs because they do not want to lose students. This academic erosion has led to a frustrated and critical attitude among state legislatures — and, consequently, less funds for state-supported schools. With the coming of reduced college and university budgets, the faculties have been forced to new levels of unionization and collective bargaining. That, in turn, has led to strikes, labor arbitration, and, more important, the loss of many talented people who leave teaching for less troubled professions. Degrees offer little evidence of competence. Few colleges require any evidence of proficiency in any subject as a requirement for a degree. "Flunking out" belongs to history.

Private higher education, caught in the pinch between the competition of public institutions and much smaller donations, has shrunk drastically. Survival has become an end in itself for many institutions. Three hundred institutions of higher education have disappeared. While the giants such as Harvard, Princeton, the University of Chicago, and Stanford still manage, we have seen the disappearance or state takeover of such fine smaller institutions as Swarthmore, Reed, Kenyon, Oberlin, and Amherst.

Another reason for the attrition of faculty is a changed age balance among the members. Twenty years ago, the average age of tenured faculty members in a four-year institution was thirty-six to forty-five, whereas today it is fifty-six to sixty-five. More and more elderly professors are now taking advantage of federal laws against age discrimination and are staying on after sixty-five. Thus, bright, young, innovative teachers often leave the system while the old, higher-paid professors stay on. This trend is very costly in both ways. Not atypically, the modern university class may present a white male sexagenarian teaching a class made up largely of women and minority students. Teachers and institutions both recognize that their future success depends on not flunking out students. They will bend any rule, compromise any standard, to retain students.

The final effect of all this has been an aging and graying of American academia. The bright young research assistants in mathematics have gone to Fort Meade, those in electronics to Bell Laboratories, those in business school to real estate, those in economics to the Rand Corporation, and so on. There has been a brain drain away from higher education. The "fittest" don't survive: they leave for better opportunities.

We have sought to fill their places with the electronic teaching instruments of our era — computers, television, courses on cassettes, courses via satellite. The marvels of computer science have permitted many of these modes of instruction to be "interactive" — that is, the computer brain can conduct a learning dialogue with the student. But in this highly technological "classroom," we find the college dropout rate doubling every four years. There appears to be a basic need for the intellectual role model traditionally offered in the form of a living teacher. Watching *Roots* on television and playing video games are not academic exercises.

To sum up: Higher education has been drained of much of its experimentation and imagination through lowering of admission standards, dilution of grade standards, a tendency to popularize curricula, and a massive shift in favor of professional and vocational major fields. Most of our colleges and universities have receded to a high school level of quality. Gone is much of the intellectual rigor. Symbolic of this is the fact that university presidents no longer function as educators — they must be publicists, business executives, recruiters, and fund raisers. They raise money, not standards.

We are losing a very important opportunity. Between 1980 and today, there has been a 23.3 percent decline in numbers among the eighteen-to-twenty-four-year-old age group. With smaller enrollments, we should be doing a better job of education than in the past. But instead we are doing a poorer job, and, consequently, we are losing a percentage of the "leadership edge" of that generation. We submit that this will be very costly for the nation in times to come.

Law and Lawyers

St. Yves is from Brittany,
A lawyer but not a thief.
Such a thing is beyond belief.

> — a popular rhyme about a fourteenth-century
> lawyer who was made a saint because he
> represented the poor

Statement
of the Chief Justice of the Supreme Court
to the Senate Judiciary Committee
July 20, 2000

My predecessor, Chief Justice Warren Burger, once said, "We may be well on our way to a society overrun by hordes of lawyers, hungry as locusts, and brigades of judges in numbers never before contemplated."

We are no longer "well on our way." We have arrived. America has become the most litigious, lawyer-filled nation on earth.

The Legal System

One cannot review the staggering growth in the number of lawyers in America without thinking of the old Mexican curse, "May your life be filled with lawyers." The number of lawyers has doubled in the past fifteen years. We now have 1.3 million lawyers in the United States, compared to 650,000 in 1984. The current 1.3 million is six times the number of lawyers there were in 1951, twice the number of lawyers there were in 1984. On a working day in the average large American city, one out of every one hundred human beings of all ages and races is a lawyer.

More significant for the future is the fact that we now have 205 law schools (compared to 172 accredited law schools in 1984) with 200,000 students and graduating classes of 50,000 more lawyers every year.

The United States has twice as many lawyers per thousand people as England, five times as many as West Germany, twenty-five times as many as Japan. Two-thirds of all of the lawyers in the world practice in the United States. Between 1973 and 1983, lawyers' billings tripled, going from $9.9 billion to $33.9 billion, and they have increased fourfold since 1983. There are more judges in Los Angeles County, California, than in all of France. We face legal gridlock, and no person is safe from a lawsuit.

The Rand Corporation, in studying early settlements in asbestos-related lawsuits, found that for every $2.59 paid out by defendants, 95 cents went to defendants' lawyers, 64 cents went to plaintiffs' lawyers, and $1 went to victims and their families. That adds up to $1.59 for the lawyers, $1 for the folks. Another study showed that plaintiffs' lawyers took 35 cents out of every dollar the plaintiffs recovered, and defendants' lawyers got an additional 45 cents from defending the same litigation. Nine out of ten cases are settled out of court and never go to trial, but lawyers are present on both sides, compounding the inefficiencies.

Lawyers have almost ceased to be healers of conflict. Instead they more often add a surcharge on misery and conflict. Our legal system encourages adversarial legal action, is awash with inefficiencies and complexities, and is the slowest, most expensive, and most complex legal system in the world. As Ambrose Bierce defined it, a lawsuit is "a machine which you go into as a pig and come out as a sausage." It has painfully little to do with justice.

The Litigious Society

That the United States has more lawyers per capita than other nations is explained by the fact that we are one of the most litigious of societies. State filings have increased five to seven times faster than population and are on a course such that if they were to continue, we would find civil filings doubling every thirteen and a half years and criminal filings doubling every eleven years. This would put an immense strain on America's economy.

Federal courts have a similar increase in burden. They received about one hundred fifty thousand suits annually in 1980 and two hundred fifty thousand a year by the end of the century. But the rate of lawsuits filed in federal courts continues to increase and today the federal appellate courts alone hear one million cases a year. The total number of lawsuits in the federal courts seems to be growing at an astounding rate. It is estimated that the United States is 25 percent more litigious than West Germany and 30 to 40 percent more litigious than Sweden. Lawrence H. Silberman, a former deputy attorney general of the United States, has said, "The legal process, because of its unbridled growth, has become a cancer which threatens the vitality of our forms of capitalism and democracy."

Alexander Solzhenitsyn, in his 1978 Harvard commencement address, observed, "The defense of individual rights has reached such extremes as to make society as a whole defenseless against certain individuals." The law protects criminals but not citizens.

It is estimated that the United States is not only the most litigious society, but that probably 90 percent of the world's criminal jury trials are held in the United States and that some 98 percent of all civil jury trials are held in the United States.

In short, America suffers under what can be called "legalflation," which threatens the efficiency and justice of our system.

International Traumas

Civilizations die of suicide, not by murder.

— Arnold Toynbee

Memorandum

To: The President
From: The Secretary of Agriculture
Re: Infinite Needs; Finite Supply
Date: December 20, 2000

At the risk of being labeled the Scrooge of your administration this Christmas season, I recommend that we make no grain shipments to the famine areas, but instead concentrate our relief in those countries that have a long-term possibility of feeding themselves. I believe we should accept the fact that food is a tool of international diplomacy. America can hardly support its own welfare load, and we now find that we are on the verge of having our own permanent international welfare load.

Our International Welfare Load

Simply put, the United States finds itself, in the year 2000, with an international welfare load to match its domestic welfare load, and both of these are expanding dramatically. The root cause of the foreign obligation was, in some instances, economic instability, in others demographic instability, and in yet others political instability. But the net result has been the same: a compassionate United States undertook, for the best of motives, a "temporary help" that did not turn out to be temporary at all. Looking back on it, one is amazed that we could have deluded ourselves that it ever would have been temporary. The conditions that we were attempting to alleviate were not temporary but were obviously long-lasting, and our lack of hard analysis led us to make commitments that now are impossible to continue. First, let us look at the welfare load caused by the demographic crisis.

Africa

In the 1980s and 1990s, Africa suffered a series of converging crises, any one of which, taken alone, might have been resolved. But happening simultaneously, they brought inevitable chaos, poverty, starvation, and political revolution. Population growth drained resources needed to revitalize the economy. Political instability prevented industrialization and economic growth, which prevented programs to control population (Africa has the lowest contraceptive use of any continent). Political instability also hampered use of Africa's many natural resources, which in turn brought economic collapse. Urban migration swelled cities to unmanageable sizes; social services broke down; education, never fully rooted, disappeared; tribalism prevented cooperation and encouraged fertility races, competition among tribes to expand their populations; and drought and overutilization of land frustrated any hope of agricultural self-sufficiency.

Africa now has a population of 740 million, up from 513 million in 1983. There are 20 million new hungry mouths to feed in Africa *every year,* whereas in North America, with a much superior agricultural base, we add only 3 million people a year. Even without drought, this was a prescription for disaster.

Africa, at a rate of 3 percent a year, is the fastest-growing continent in the world — having doubled its population in less than twenty-five years. Back in 1984, of the United Nations Population Assistance priority countries, thirty-three out of fifty-three were in Africa. Of the world's poorest countries, twenty-three of the thirty-five were in Africa, and these twenty-three had a per capita income of $500 per year. All these statistics have worsened since then.

The death rate, in classic Malthusian fashion, once kept Africa's population in check. Between 1650 and the 1900s, the continent's population remained almost static while Europe grew fourfold. Africa practiced death control rather than birth control. Since the independence era of the 1960s, few African nations have shown the political stability to develop their resources, and the result is chaos.

We find today, then, that sub-Saharan Africa and Southeast Asia contain the world's poorest countries with the fastest-growing populations. They accounted for 35 percent of the world's population in 1980. They make up 45 percent today. They will constitute 60 percent by the year 2050. Since 1983, Europe grew by 4.5 percent, the United States grew by 14.5 percent, but Latin America grew by 44.6 percent and Africa grew by 65.9 percent. Those Third World rates are clearly unsustainable and are the direct cause of the United States' massive assistance programs that we now cannot sustain.

In the ten years previous to 1984, Africa's per capita food production was declining, and it has continued to decline. Africa had a thirteen-year drought in the 1970s and early 1980s. But even before the drought, the population growth, averaging 3 percent per year, outstripped a food supply that would grow 1.3 percent a year.

Only U.S. and European generosity has kept Africa from megafamine.

Julius Nyerere, president of Tanzania, once stated, "In one world, as in one state, when I am rich because you are poor, and I am poor because you are rich, the transfer of wealth from the rich to the poor is a matter of right."

However eloquent Nyerere's statement, this notion is politically impossible to implement and morally absurd. We did not make Africa poor. Its leaders can cite the crime of colonialism only so long. The developed nations have given every effort to helping Africa develop. We must be clearheaded about our ability to meet starvation in a world rife with hunger.

Egypt

Egypt's population in the year 2000 is 60 million, whereas in 1970 it was 32 million. Cairo, designed to hold 2.5 million people, had 8.5 million in 1984, with another 2 million jamming into the city every day to work. Today, Cairo is home to 13 million people, most of them existing at a subsistence level. Many squatters actually live in the mausoleums in Cairo's cemeteries.

Thus, the real crisis in Egypt is overpopulation and degradation of the agricultural land. According to the United Nations Food and Agriculture Organization, Egypt has less than two-tenths of one acre of arable land to support each citizen. That represents one-quarter of the world's average and is less than the arable land per capita averaged for the overwhelming majority of the nations of the world. It is obvious that Egypt's population cannot be supported on two-tenths of an acre per person. The nation used to export foodstuffs. Today it imports massive amounts of grain just to feed its population. At the present growth rate,

Egypt's 60 million people will become 78 million in about fifteen years, and instead of having two-tenths of an acre of arable land to support each citizen, it will have one-tenth of an acre.

That assumes, however, that there will be no further encroachment of the desert. Yet Egypt's available agricultural land has been shrinking by 600,000 acres per year. Forty years ago Egypt could not support its population on four times the amount of land available today. How can it do so with one-quarter of the amount of land in the future? The country will have to import, at a minimum, twice as much food as it does today, with a growing population.

Egypt needs 3 million new dwellings every year; it produces only 160,000. One person in three has inadequate accommodations. Many Cairo residents are without sanitation facilities and often without drinking water or electricity. The Moslem Brotherhood stirs discontent and it is doubtful that a secular Egyptian state can long be preserved. Egypt survives on the generosity of the developed world.

Argentina

Argentina is a classic case of a nation that could be self-sufficient but now seeks our help. In the 1930s, it was a relatively strong and vital country with a gross national product larger than Canada's, twice as high as Italy's, and almost equal to that of France. Its GNP at that time made it one of the ten most economically powerful nations.

Today, Argentina is seething with revolutionary ferment. We can observe there the same elements of political instability that have in the past caused political revolutions throughout South and Central America: a huge percentage of the wealth at the apex of a steeply sloping economic pyramid, no middle class to bridge the gap between the haves and the have-nots, and a military establishment to control the country for the benefit of the economic elite. Argentina has triple-digit inflation and an economy that doesn't work. It can feed itself, but it is broke, financially bankrupt and living on U.S. loans — though it has never repaid any loan.

Egypt and Argentina, two once-successful nations, are now examples of the plight of a Third World that we have encouraged to rely on us. Their people are resentful and angry — the tinder of revolution, the gasoline of anarchy.

We have not increased America's influence and popularity by our food aid. We have increased these nations' frustration when we ran out of "surplus" food. We have played right into revolution.

Our Shrinking Agricultural Base

While the demands on American generosity have been growing, our resources have been shrinking. The agronomist and Nobel Peace Prize winner Norman Borlaug pointed out, back in 1975, that even with dramatically reduced population growth rates the world would still have to produce more food and fiber during the next forty years than it had in the twelve thousand years since the dawn of agriculture. He further pointed out that it would have to be done after most of the best arable land, the most fertile land, and the land most blessed with good climate had already come under cultivation.

So, I do not believe that even under the best of circumstances we could have reached that objective. Perhaps if everything had gone right we would have had a chance. But that issue is academic.

The fact is, everything did not go right. The world, tragically, has turned its topsoil, which was a renewable resource, into a nonrenewable resource. We knew for some time that in many parts of the world the topsoil was being blown away, contaminated, exhausted, and abused for a quick profit. In 1983, two billion acres of the world were desert. Now, only seventeen years later, that figure has doubled. In the United States, which was the globe's leading agricultural country, the severe soil losses have made 12 percent of our cropland and 17 percent of our rangeland unproductive.

The world's food depends upon farmland, which, for many years, has been disappearing from this planet at an alarming rate. Like oil, of course, when it is gone, it is gone. We have ignored the many signs of widespread topsoil depletion just as we ignored the first signs of the energy crisis. The reasons vary from place to place, but the result is the same — a substantial loss of the world's agricultural capacity.

It would pay us to look at the causes. In some countries — the United States, for instance — there was the conversion of prime agricultural farmland to other uses. Along with most of the rest of the world, the United States experienced serious soil erosion and loss of fertility. In much of the world, the undesirable patterns of agricultural ownership, with a small percentage of the landowners owning a large percentage of the land, were a factor.

In other areas the cause was drought and climate change, and in still others it was water scarcity. In much of the world, energy shortages and high costs hurt the agriculture, and in other areas genetic overspecialization and vulnerability of crops were the problem. Whatever the reason, the result was the same — a dramatic loss in the agricultural capacity that was not offset by the agricultural advances that have been made.

U.S. agricultural productivity has been astounding. Despite the loss of agricultural land, our productivity has increased. Drought-resistant and insect-resistant grains need no spraying and many can now grow in saline soil. Genetic engineering allows us to twin all livestock pregnancies so that we double production. Growth hormones in dairy cattle give us 20 percent more production on top of an existing surplus. Many of these technologies have improved agricultural productivity in other parts of the world. But the areas of the world that need our surplus food can't afford to purchase it. We can give away endless quantities, but our challenge is to find paying customers. Even paying customers, however, result in the erosion of our soil base.

Exports of grain and soybeans have been increasing rampantly in the last forty years. In 1950, we exported 15 tons of grain as compared with 119 million tons in 1983 and 150 million tons in 1988. The biggest growth has come in corn and soybeans, including processed soybean meal, which is a staple of meat, poultry, egg, and milk production. Soybean exports more than tripled in the 1960s, and in the 1970s feedgrain exports increased sevenfold. Back in 1984 we exported more than 60 percent of our wheat; more than half of our soybeans, cotton, rice; nearly a third of our corn. I am not pretending that this was done altruistically. It was done for good old-fashioned economic reasons. In fact, one University of Minnesota economist said, "In terms of competition for land, we have reached a degree of agricultural export dependency for which parallels can be found only in the ante-bellum cotton South, or in our colonial era." The exports and other demands for food increased the pressure on the land and made it more susceptible to erosion. We have had substantial erosion in many parts of the United States, by both water and wind, but worse is the washing away of hilly land brought into row crop cultivation in response to the high prices of corn and beans.

If we want American agriculture to continue producing its enormous volume in the future, we must act now to stop the deterioration of the soil base. That means a cutback in the production of grain and soybeans. It is now very clear that we are in danger of overexploiting much of our farmland in order to keep on increasing our export of grain — and, in fact, we have already ruined some of the best land in the world in this way.

The reasons for this historic error are, obviously, twofold. Back in the 1970s, we began to sell large amounts of agricultural products to the Soviet Union and many other nations. Since then, we have had a series of short-term economic incentives of the same sort, as country after country lost the race between population growth and agricultural growth. More recently we have had, instead of a controlled sale to customer nations, a demanded export to starving nations. The first great example, of course, was that of Ethiopia in the 1980s. Since then, Third World nation after nation has come to us with its heart-rending pictures of starving babies and dying mothers.

This administration faces an impossible request. America simply cannot feed the whole world. Even with the all-out food production that would surely destroy our soil resources within a few decades, we could not be the granary for a world of exploding populations. Painful as the decision is, we cannot condemn our own descendants to hunger in order to try to do an impossible job in the rest of the world today. The only answer is to try to help those countries that are willing to increase their own food production by modern methods.

The United States has sent the wrong signals for the last thirty years about our capacity to provide food relief. We assumed, in the United States, that we could feed the world, and we had a supply-side agricultural policy that turned out to be as mistaken as our supply-side energy policy. We now understand, realistically, that we cannot do the impossible. The world's population in 1984 was 4.6 billion. Today it is 5.6 billion. It is projected to grow to 10.3 billion by the year 2050. The population of the industrialized countries, however, will only be 1.5 billion in the year 2050, while the developing world will grow from 4.4 billion today to almost 9 billion.

Our projections for 2050, which have their genesis in figures released by the World Bank back in 1984, was that India's population will reach 1.8 billion, making it the most populous nation on earth. Bangladesh, a nation the size of our state of Wisconsin, is projected to have a population of 430 million. Nigeria, Ethiopia, Zaire, and Kenya are together projected to have populations of almost 1.2 billion.

The best description, Madam President, of the abject poverty that these nations suffer I found in Robert L. Heilbroner's 1963 book *The Great Ascent: The Struggle for Economic Development in Our Time.* He described what we would have to do to reduce the circumstances of the average American family to those of a Third World family.

We begin by invading the house to strip it of its furniture. Everything goes: beds, chairs, tables, television set. We will leave the family with a few old blankets, a kitchen table, a wooden chair . . . The box of matches may stay, a small bag of flour, some sugar and salt. A few moldy potatoes already in the garbage can must be rescued, for they will provide much of tonight's meal.

The bathroom is dismantled, the running water shut off, the electric wires taken out. Next, we take away the house. The family can move to the toolshed. Communications must go next. No more newspapers, magazines, books . . . Next, government services must go. No more postmen, no more firemen. There is a school, but it is three miles

away and consists of two rooms. They are not too over-
crowded since only half the children in the neighborhood
go to school.

The nearest clinic is ten miles away and is tended by a
midwife. It can be reached by bicycle provided the family
has a bicycle, which is unlikely . . . Finally, money. We will
allow our family a cash hoard of $5 . . .

Madam President, the suffering is great but our resources are overtaxed. We can make ourselves poor, but we
cannot make other countries rich.

It is thus my recommendation that we use our small
surplus of food as a diplomatic tool where it can best advance the interests of the United States. We cannot continue to support both a domestic and an international welfare load.

Madam President, we live with agonizing choices. We
cannot do everything, yet we want to do something. My
point is that that "something" can often be worse than
nothing. A number of years ago, a DC-10, on a flight from
Málaga to New York, was just taking off. At about thirty feet
above the runway the pilot felt "something was radically
wrong" and aborted the takeoff. The crash landing killed
fifty people, while all the others escaped by the emergency
exits. The pilot said, after the crash, "I don't know if I killed
fifty people or saved two hundred."

Madam President, I do know. We cannot feed the world.
Our aid must be for temporary relief, not a permanent
welfare load. It is our only political and moral option.

The Sin of Softheartedness:
A Sermon by the Right Rev. Robert King,
Episcopal Bishop of Southern Ohio
June 1999

I preach this morning of reality theology and triage ethics. Let me share with you the parable of Juan Fernandes as told by Joseph Townsend in 1786.

> In the South Seas there is an island, which from the first discoverer is called Juan Fernandes. In this sequestered spot John Fernando placed a colony of goats consisting of one male attended by his female. This happy couple, finding pasture in abundance, could readily obey the first commandment, to increase and multiply, till in process of time they had replenished the little island . . . From this unhappy moment they began to suffer hunger . . . When the Spaniards found that the English privateers resorted to this island for provisions, they resolved on the total extirpation of the goats, and for this purpose they put on shore a greyhound dog and bitch. These in their turn increased and multiplied, in proportion to the quantity of food they met with; but in consequence, as the Spaniards had foreseen, the herd of goats diminished. Had they been totally destroyed, the dogs likely must have perished. But as many of the goats retired to the craggy rocks, where the dogs could never follow them, descending only for short intervals to feed with fear and circumspection in the valleys, none but the most watchful, strong and active of the dogs could get a sufficiency of food. Thus a new kind of balance was established.

The world, like the island of Juan Fernandes, is undergoing a new kind of balance. I have come to the sad conclusion that it needs both goats and dogs. The famines now sweeping the globe are God's way of reasserting balance. "Suffer the little children to come unto me, and forbid them not; for of such is the kingdom of God."

Did we really think we could grow indefinitely both in population and economically? It just wasn't possible.

Let us look at the human predicament from another viewpoint. John McPhee stated it so well in *Encounters with the Archdruid:*

> Compare the six days of Genesis as a figure of speech for what has in fact been four billion years geologic time. On this scale, a day equals something like 666 million years and thus:
>
> All day Monday until Tuesday noon, Creation was busy getting the earth going. Life began Tuesday noon and the beautiful organic wholeness of it developed over the next four days. At 4 p.m. Saturday, the big reptiles came. Five hours later, when the redwoods appeared, there were no more big reptiles. At three minutes before midnight Man appeared and one-fourth of a second before midnight Christ arrived. At one-fortieth of a second before midnight, the Industrial Revolution began.
>
> We are surrounded by people who think that what we have been doing for one-fortieth of a second can go on indefinitely. They are considered normal, but they are stark raving mad.

Some of you object to how I have changed the biblical quote from "Love thy neighbor" to "Love thy nearest neighbor." You ask how a church with a tradition of missionaries and universal caring could love only thy nearest neighbor. You object to my concept of "toughlove," in which we simply accept the starvation in much of the Third

World. You ask, "How can I ignore those pitiful scenes of megafamine that we see on our televisions every day?"

It is my sad and reluctant conclusion that the economy within the United States cannot keep up with all the problems outside its borders and that we were foolish to try. It is my conclusion that "toughlove" means that we let God's judgment take place in much of the Third World and that by trying to relieve this suffering all we do is postpone it.

To them we say, with Jeremiah 2:7:

> And I brought you into a plentiful land
> to enjoy its fruits and its good things.
> But when you came in you defiled my land,
> and made my heritage an abomination.

And 4:18:

> Your ways and your doings
> have brought this upon you.
> This is your doom, and it is bitter;
> it has reached your very heart.

Even if these countries had the capital, knowledge, and skills to become "developed" countries — which they don't — the world does not have the resources to give everyone a "developed country" standard of living. It would put an unbearable drain on the world's finite resources. To raise per capita energy consumption to the U.S. level, the world would need to burn 300 percent more coal, 500 percent more petroleum, and 1100 percent more natural gas. To believe that this will happen is more than wishful thinking; it belongs to the Our Lady of Lourdes school of politics.

Alas, we had both a lifeboat and a *Titanic* — and both are now sinking.

Our civilization has been running a marathon as if it were a hundred-yard dash. We thought the earth limitless, and even after the astronauts brought back their marvelous pictures of the finite globe we all share, we continued to act as if we could endlessly abuse it. Albert Schweitzer warned us, "We have lost the ability to foresee and forestall. We shall end by destroying the earth."

Alas, we didn't listen. Each year our population grows; the deserts creep; the pollution seeps; the forests shrink; topsoil erodes; habitats degrade; and more species disappear. We are destroying the earth that we rely on for life; we are consuming our seed corn; we are treating our one-time inheritance of capital as if it were interest. We are blind to our excesses and deaf to all the evidence.

Aristotle said it so well: "From time to time it is necessary that pestilence, famine and war prune the luxuriant growth of the human race." Thus your argument isn't with me. It's with nature.

Just as "God is dead" theology failed because it had an unwinnable argument with God, so did liberation theology fail because it had an unwinnable argument with nature.

Reality theology is a revolution in human thought. I do not claim it is the best scenario; far better had we listened to Schweitzer and learned to "foresee and forestall." Alas, we didn't — and now we are left with no other practical alternatives. The stork has become a bird of prey. Chaos is on the march. Triage ethics always stand by, dictated by nature, to push out all other ethical standards that fail. It is theological Darwinism: if your ethics don't jibe with reality, my ethics will. Just as triage is blessed in time of war, reality theology will be blessed in a time of chaos.

We have thoughtlessly destroyed one million species in the last ten years, the products of twenty million centuries of evolution.

We ethnocentrically thought the earth belonged to us. But, alas, ecologically we belong to the earth. And the earth is now claiming its due from a myopic species called man.

As we are clearly unable to alleviate all suffering and starvation, we have a Christian responsibility to use both our hearts and our heads to maximize the good we can do. Those answers, however, as with triage during war, are unorthodox and would require a change in policy for most of organized religion. But we cannot escape the task.

Write me a "happy" scenario for Bangladesh. Show me a happy outcome, a nice solution for a poverty-wracked country that has 90 million people crowded into an area the size of Iowa. An average Bangladeshi woman has fourteen pregnancies, produces 6.5 children. More than 60 percent of all women in that country have seven or more children. Many women are pregnant twenty-four times or more, and it is common to see a woman of thirty with eight living children and seven grandchildren. Please, my mind just doesn't see it. What is the happy ending?

Give me a scenario of social justice in Mexico City in the year 2000 with 30 million people in a cramped, polluted basin; or Calcutta with 20 million; or Cairo, Teheran, or Karachi with 14 to 16 million. Does God give a prize to the city with the largest number of deserving poor? Can we both liberate and multiply the poor? Paint me an acceptable picture when we have Third World populations with over 40 percent under sixteen years of age packed into shantytowns and barrios without adequate health or housing. There are now fifty-eight cities with over 5 million people, compared to twenty-nine such cities in 1984, most of them filled with poor, uneducated, unskilled people in a pressure cooker of social and economic stress.

Write me a "Christian" scenario for these realities. There is none. That's why reality theology adopted its "toughlove" philosophy. That's why triage ethics is, in the long run, the most compassionate.

Consider two countries, India and China. Massive amounts of aid from America and other developed countries have gone to India. At one time a ship of supplies per day arrived in India to help alleviate hunger. What has this effort brought India? People there live on the near end of misery and poverty.

On the other hand, China essentially received no foreign assistance after the Soviet Union terminated its aid in 1960. It relied upon no country, for it had none to rely upon. It came to grips with its own problems without becoming an international welfare case.

Now I ask you, which nation is better off today, India or China?

This society and this church have suffered from too much blind optimism and not enough clear-eyed realism. Our values and our theologies were structured in a different time and in a different era, under different pressures. Thus, our perceptions of reality lag far behind the actual reality. We have a hard time keeping our moral compasses steady because supposed "solutions" and alternatives disappear before our very eyes. Yesterday's generosity and emergency aid have become today's "international obligation." But the new reality is that we cannot save all the starving children; we cannot help significant numbers without ruining our own economy; we see ambitious people who want to come to the United States but we cannot accept them all; we see children who need new kidneys and elderly who could use a heart transplant, but the reality is that the demand and cost of these procedures exceed our resources. Triage ethics and reality theology wait in the wings to justify what softer and more naive theologies thought of as drastic remedies. As at other times in history, the church must eventually bless what people do to survive.

I realize we have no political language, no moral codes, and no philosophical tenets to equip us for the choices that we are faced with and that we are having to make on a day-to-day basis.

The redistribution of U.S. wealth would not make anybody rich. It would simply make us all poor. It is not heresy to point out that we should help other nations feed their own, but we cannot and should not take that task upon our own nation.

Somewhere along the line we must say no, and ironically, the earlier we say it, the fewer people will be hurt.

We all know the story of St. Martin of Tours, who gave away half his cloak to a naked beggar he met on the road. This has become a marvelous symbol of generosity and sharing, and it is part of our heritage. But the new relative analogy that we must consider is if St. Martin, instead of meeting one beggar, had met twenty naked and starving beggars on his path. Would he have cut his cloak into twenty inadequate pieces? How would he have chosen among the 20 deserving beggars? What standards and what values would he have brought to that decision?

A number of years ago, the *New York Times* carried a story that is a metaphor for reality theology. An American nun in Bangladesh, after a couple of days in the country, found a starving baby on her doorstep. She took in the baby, fed it, and clothed it. The following morning there was another starving baby on her doorstep. She gave that one shelter and clothing also. On the third day she was confronted with yet another starving baby. Finally, her order told her to stop taking in the starving babies. The task was too immense, the numbers too gargantuan. "Leave them on the doorstep," ordered her superior.

Nothing in our Christian tradition can give us guidelines for these kinds of agonizing decisions. Our moral compasses gyrate wildly, but the issue will not go away.

The intellectual civil war that goes on within me is trying to deal with the immense questions that my political training sees cannot be avoided. I have neither a cloistered virtue nor a cloistered ethical standard. I am trying to reconcile ancient values with the new, shattering, and terrifying reality with which I am faced.

You charge me with heresy for having "triage ethics" and exposing the "sins of softheartedness." But what are the moral alternatives?

Professor Van Rensselaer Potter, the widely respected oncologist, in his 1971 book *Bioethics: Bridge to the Future,* stated it so well:

> What we must now face up to is the fact that human ethics cannot be separated from a realistic understanding of ecology in the broadest sense. *Ethical values* cannot be separated from *biological facts.* We are in great need of a Land Ethic, a Wildlife Ethic, a Population Ethic, a Consumption Ethic, an Urban Ethic, an International Ethic, a Geriatric Ethic, and so on. All of these problems call for actions that are based on values *and* biological facts. All of them involve Bioethics, and survival of the total ecosystem is the test of the value system.
>
> The age-old questions about the nature of man and his relation to the world become increasingly important . . . when political decisions made in ignorance of biological knowledge, or in defiance of it, may jeopardize man's future and indeed the future of earth's biological resources for human needs.

The greatest misperception that Western man has ever entertained is that he is separate from nature and that he can control and exploit it for his material well-being. Human dominion over the earth means all living things will inevitably end in tragedy. We have ended up destroying our ecosystems, quadrupling the rate of extinction of the animals. The world has changed more in the last thirty years than it did from the time of Christ to 1950. Our institutional memory is at variance with the reality we face.

The failure to recognize the human relationship to nature will be traumatic — and even fatal — to millions of people. It will trigger change equal to a worldwide Dark Age. A new world will develop and a new civilization will recognize, as did the American Indians, that we need to live in harmony with nature and Mother Earth.

You call my attitude on this heartless; nature is similarly heartless. Is the lion that kills the zebras heartless? The wolves that cull the old, lame, and sick from a caribou herd heartless? No. They simply are following the demands of nature. Nature will ultimately demand that humans cease to exceed the earth's carrying capacity — it is now happening. But we are trying to stop the tide, trying to stop winter from arriving, trying to stop human death. Ultimately, we are children both of God and nature. Humankind comes with the same warranty that the dinosaurs had.

The theologian Wolfhart Pannenberg once said, "The real danger in faith lies in its estrangement from rationality." I believe this church has not adapted its thinking to the realities of a world of six billion people awash with poverty and starvation. My remedies may seem harsh, but I feel that all the possible easy remedies of the 1960s, 1970s, and 1980s were ignored. A world of scarce resources makes hard choices not only necessary but inevitable.

Memorandum

To: The President
From: The Secretary of State
Re: The Balance of Power
Date: July 4, 2000

Madam President, let's first look at the condition of the USSR to see how she has fared since the Second World War. A significant case can be made that what we are seeing is the slow dissolution of the Soviet empire, not, by the way, due to anything that we have done, but because of her internal dynamics. When seen through her own eyes, the Soviet Union is beset by myriad problems. She has a billion Chinese who despise her on one border. She is fighting an unwinnable war in Afghanistan that increasingly drains her resources and youth. She has Solidarity in Poland and a revolution of rising expectations throughout the Eastern bloc countries, where dissent is always hovering just below the surface. She forced a number of countries — Latvia, Lithuania, the Ukraine — into her political and economic system, and many of those people hate this subjugation with a passion. She has an economy that does not work.

The Soviet Union has forty million Moslems who have a birthrate five times that of ethnic Russians. Combining the Moslems with other nationalities such as the Latvians, Kazakhs, Uighurs, Azerbaijanis, Lithuanians, and Turkmenians, we find that soon ethnic white Russians will be a minority within the Soviet Union. The average age of the Soviet population is increasing, and increasingly the government is having to rely on these minority nationalities to fill its armies. These people are often non-Russian-speaking and non-Slavic-speaking. In short, Russia is an aging empire, full of strains and stresses.

It is my belief that too many leaders throughout our history, in every realm, have failed to adequately understand the meaning of new circumstances thrust upon them. That is why we had cavalry charges against machine gun positions as late as the First World War; generations of military strategists just could not believe that the cavalry charge was obsolete. We then found a new and equally blind strategy of warfare developing that in turn did not incorporate the tank and the power of the new technologies that Hitler so well understood and De Gaulle, almost alone among the Allies, recognized.

It is true that generals always prepare for the last war. We get in a mode of thinking about a certain set of circumstances and it becomes very difficult, if not impossible, for us to thrust out of that thought pattern and see the circumstances of the new world in which we live. Great leaders are those who challenge conventional wisdom, who think the unthinkable, and who throw over the existing assumptions. The hardest thing to do in politics is to change a policy that has been branded successful. One fights past successes, inertia, and skepticism. Yet it is absolutely essential that each generation correctly appraise the realities with which it is faced.

It is thus my assertion, Madam President, that we must adopt policies to face the new realities of our times. It is my contention that we have built, in this country, a Maginot Line. We and the Russians have together achieved grotesque levels of redundancy of nuclear weapons and each technological advance makes us less safe, not more.

What this massive transfer of wealth into defense spending has meant, however, is a serious undercutting of the American economy. Whereas Japan spent 0.5 percent of its gross national product on defense, we have spent approximately 7 percent, year in and year out, for the last thirty years, part of it to protect Japan. Thus, 40 percent of our engineers and physicists have gone into defense work, while the Japanese apply virtually all their talent and dedication to dominating markets and expanding their worldwide market share. We, in the meantime, have built a terrific military machine, but it is at the price of our economy.

Dwight D. Eisenhower warned, "The problem in defense is how far you can go without destroying from within that which you are trying to defend from without." That statement still applies. Our trade deficit is not with the Soviet Union. The predatory pricing mechanisms that keep out American goods and dump foreign goods in this country have not been caused by the Russians. On the contrary, a case can be made that our friends have done us more harm in the last twenty years than our enemies.

The Resource War

The United States is also finding that it is more vulnerable to a resource war than was ever felt possible before. In certain crucial minerals and metals, a declining domestic capacity, combined with an increasing domestic use, has been offset by an increase in mineral imports. This greater reliance upon foreign sources has brought forth the OPEC-style cartels. While many of these cartels have failed owing to vast differences among producer nations and political, social, and economic strategies in certain key metals and minerals, the United States has become dangerously dependent upon these foreign sources.

A 1980 study on U.S. import dependence of eight minerals hauntingly previewed the resource war that we find ourselves in. The results of that study are shown here.

U.S. Import Dependence: Eight Key Minerals

Material	Import Reliance (Percent of Total Consumption)	Major Import Source(s)
Chromium	92%	USSR, South Africa
Cobalt	97%	South Africa
Platinum-group metals	91%	South Africa, USSR
Columbium	100%	Brazil, Thailand, Nigeria, Malaysia
Fluorspar	82%	South Africa
Manganese	98%	Gabon, South Africa
Bauxite	93%	Jamaica, Australia, Surinam, Guinea
Titanium	*	USSR is the largest producer of titanium "sponge," the semiprocessed metal. Japan, Britain, and China also produce titanium sponge. Canada and Australia are major producers of titanium ore.

*Import reliance withheld to avoid disclosing individual company confidential data.

Source: "The Resource War and the U.S. Business Community: The Case for a Council on Economics and National Security," CENS, Washington, D.C.

In the last twenty years, our consumption patterns have made us highly vulnerable to the resource war we now find ourselves in. When the United States consumes one-third of the world's energy, with American automobiles using one-ninth of all the world's petroleum, we find ourselves in an exposed position. Even more markedly, America's mineral industry has become increasingly dependent upon foreign production, and we find ourselves vulnerable in another strategic area.

The United States, for the last twenty years, has imported 93 percent of its platinum from southern Africa, as well as 42 percent of its magnesium, 76 percent of its cobalt, and 48 percent of its chromium.

It was twenty years ago that a congressional committee found, "Without chromium or cobalt we cannot build an automobile, a computer, a cutting tool, or other high-technology equipment. We could not run a train nor process food under present laws and we cannot build an oil refinery or power station."

We recognize now the interdependent relationships between our military security, our economic security, and our raw material needs.

Former Secretary of State Alexander Haig warned of this resource war back in 1980, when he stated, "Should future trends, especially in Africa, result in an alignment with Moscow of this critical resource area, then the USSR would control as much as 90 percent of several key minerals for which no substitute has been developed."

These minerals and metals are strategically important to a complex industrial society such as the United States.

Thus we find that U.S. energy and mineral destiny has been tied to the two most anachronistic areas in the world: Saudi Arabia and southern Africa.

A new equation has thus been added to the geopolitical forces of the world — the power to control and thus to deny critical metals and minerals. The country that can control, or have its surrogates control, the flow of these critical minerals literally has the power to bring another nation to its knees.

These shutoffs are not subject to either gunboat diplomacy or dollar diplomacy.

Crisis: Problems Outrunning Solutions

It behooves us to consider seriously the possibility of intentionally stopping growth ourselves and of adjusting our ways of life to accommodate to this new situation . . . Society should continue to evolve century after century, but within the framework of a stabilized population and constant per capita consumption of energy and other raw materials.

— Harrison Brown, *The Human Future Revisited* (1978)

Letter of Resignation of
the Secretary of Energy
November 10, 2000

Madam President:

My heartfelt congratulations on your re-election. The voters reaffirmed your agenda of hard choices and I am honored to have played a small role in your far-sighted administration.

Sadly, however, I must tender my resignation as secretary of energy. I have ruined both my marriage and my health in attempting to come up with some "solutions" to our new energy crisis. I have failed.

I take some solace from the fact that the problem has grown no worse. Our Energy Rationing Act was implemented with a minimum of disruption and backlash. Our Mandatory Conservation Act is being accepted reluctantly.

America, in my mind, simply didn't start early enough to face the crisis. Ever since the first OPEC oil embargo of 1973 we should have known that energy was both in short supply and sure to be used as a political weapon. We ignored all the warning signs.

No secretary of energy and no administration can make up in four years for thirty years of myopia.

As you said in your first State of the Union Message, we were foolish to rely on the Middle East for a major part of the free world's oil. Since 1974, the Middle East has been a political Mount Saint Helens, waiting to blow. The question wasn't "if" it would blow up, but "when?" We have seen a sweeping Islamic revolution, a royal family in Saudi Arabia with billions of dollars in oil royalties and one-third of its work force foreign workers; a long-lived, disruptive Ayatollah Khomeini, multiple internecine Arab to Arab wars, and the Israeli/Arab conflict. It is surprising that the disruption was so late in coming. It was as inevitable as any contemporary geopolitical event.

Now we must make up for thirty years of myopia and inaction.

I wish you luck and success in your new term. If anyone can do it, you can.

Memorandum

To: The President
From: The Commanding Officer, U.S. Army Corps
        of Engineers
Re: The Water Crisis
Date: July 1, 2000

As water demand outruns supply, great areas of the world, including much of the United States, come closer and closer to catastrophic droughts.

Americans in the southern and eastern states and most Western Europeans, who enjoy an average rainfall of between 20 and 60 inches a year, find this kind of crisis hard to comprehend. For example, Athens is the only European city with an average rainfall as low as 15 inches per year.

Albuquerque, Phoenix, Salt Lake City, Las Vegas, Boise, Cheyenne, and Bismarck — and the vast western areas surrounding them — get no more, and, in some cases, even less. Viewing the world as a whole, we can predict with some certainty a global crisis in the near future. Both the Economic Commission for Europe and the U.S. Water Resources Council project severe water shortages within this decade.

The growth in demand for water is directly linked with the sharp increase in world population that has created a rising need for foodstuff. To feed their new millions, many nations have had to extend irrigation agriculture into fragile, semidesert lands and, simultaneously, to intensify the production from fertile, traditionally arable land.

The experience of the American West over the past fifty years is something of a warning for many arid regions in the rest of the world. Arizona, for example, has been drawing water from its aquifers at the rate of some 2 million acre feet a year. This is intensive exploitation. It means that, in many parts of the West, the water now being pumped sank beneath the earth from 200 million to 70 million years ago. Once exhausted, these ancient reservoirs will not fill again. With the lowering of water tables, even the land itself is beginning to sink in places, and the cost of pumping is dramatically on the rise. To add to this trouble, many surface or just subsurface water sources are becoming contaminated with salts and minerals.

For the United States as a whole, reserves are diminishing more slowly but just as steadily. Each year, rainfall replaces no more than three-quarters of the groundwater we withdraw in that time. We are borrowing from a store of natural capital and the day of dry bankruptcy lies somewhere ahead.

Even in China, with a 20- to 40-inch average annual

rainfall, and in the Soviet Union, with 20 to 40 inches in most of the European area, extensive water projects and new irrigation systems are under way. Many Near Eastern countries are in chronic need; Egypt did not meet the demands of its population growth by means of the Aswan Dam. Drought and famine have turned the upper tier of Africa from the Atlantic to the Red Sea into a parched no man's land.

The only sign of hope comes from our own incompetence. The U.S. General Accounting Office has produced a careful study pointing to the conclusion that half of the water used in American agriculture is wasted — that is, not efficiently applied to the raising of crops or the requirements of stock. In lesser percentages, this waste is permitted in agriculture throughout the world.

One of the root causes of the worsening situation has been a change in the composition of the atmosphere. Carbon dioxide, or CO_2, is one of the gases that play an important part in determining the nature of the earth's climate. It is formed by the combustion of wood, coal, or fossil fuels and it is taken from the air by plant life. As we have continued to deforest the world and to produce greater and greater amounts of CO_2, the imbalance has led to an excess, which in turn has led to a warming of the world's surface air by somewhere between 1.5 and 2.5 degrees centigrade. The result, in the United States, has been a warmer and drier climate in the major agricultural areas.

It is too soon to make any certain prediction about the long-term impact — whether or not our agriculture can adjust to the new conditions. The certain facts are that we have already begun to see a lessening of rain flow, of river flow, and of sea levels. The changes are most noticeable in the Texas Gulf, the Rio Grande, and the upper and lower Colorado River systems. There have been substantial effects in California and other western states. Some climatologists have projected a loss of nearly 50 percent of the water supply in these areas within the next two decades, which would mean that much of the irrigated farmland would have to be abandoned.

I respectfully submit that this administration must face the fact that the habitable, agriculturally productive part of America is likely to shrink drastically in the near future.

Memorandum

To: The President
From: The Secretary of Labor
Re: The Jobs Drought
Date: August 2000

There is a new scarce and precious resource in the world, and that is jobs. The implications of this scarcity and the traumas that it has already brought to society and will clearly bring in the future are immense and must be dealt with. But this administration has few realistic options. We have inherited chaos.

Let's first look at the growth in the world's labor force in the last thirty years.

Growth in the World Labor Force (in millions)

	1970	2000	Additional Jobs Required	Percent Change
More-Developed Nations	488	649	161	+33%
Less-Developed Nations	1011	1933	922	+91%

Source: Michael S. Teitelbaum, "Right vs. Right" (*Foreign Affairs*, Fall 1980).

As we can see from the above chart, the more-developed nations, with two-thirds of the gross world product, had difficulty enough finding jobs for 161 million additional people. But it was absolute chaos for the less-developed world to fail in its attempt to find 922 million new jobs with only a third of the gross world product. Jobs have become the world's scarcest resource.

Everywhere we look, we see far more applicants than available jobs. Mexico, with a comparatively small economic base, has for ten years had as many young people entering the job market each year as did the United States. Jobs need capital, and this phenomenal increase in the number of people seeking jobs came at just the time when it was hard to raise capital. India has 150,000 new entrants into its labor force every week, and it has hardly had the resources to feed them, let alone to find them jobs.

In 1950, Latin America had 55 million workers. By 1975 it had 97 million, and today it has 197 million. Latin America has, hypothetically, needed an increase of 4 million jobs a year, but of course its economy couldn't come close to supporting that. Through the 1970s and the 1980s, the

United States averaged only 2 million new jobs a year, and this was with the world's most productive economy.

The combined labor force of Mexico and Central America has doubled since 1975 and now stands at 52.6 million. In twenty-five years it is estimated to be 89.4 million. That means that the nations of this area must have found and continue to find 1.2 million jobs a year since the early 1980s. But the entire area's economy is only 8 percent as large as that of the United States. The impossibility of creating enough jobs to fill the need is obvious.

The country officials who manage scarce resources and increasingly undercut economies are striving, valiantly but fruitlessly, to keep up with exploding job demands. There simply never has been enough capital to have provided those jobs, but the governments went blindly forward, ignoring the implications of the exploding labor force. There is no revolutionary force on earth more powerful than the frustration of rising expectations combined with the inability to fulfill those expectations. The peoples of most of the Third World now live in marginal economic conditions with violence all around them, gripped by starvation and political unrest.

Unemployment in the United States

There has also been massive unemployment in the United States, owing to a number of factors.

Illegal immigration is one. Our economy in the last thirty years averaged 2.002 million new jobs annually, but our lack of control of our borders allowed 2 million legal and illegal immigrants to settle in the United States every year. That caused unemployment to rise to 15.2 percent by 1990 and to 19.1 percent by this year. We have added the equivalent of another California to our population in the last sixteen years. Our population is now 300 million and our resources are not adequate to find jobs even for our own people. We now watch the fading of the American Dream.

America is losing its middle class. We have also found, in the last twenty years, that a number of workers have skidded down the occupational ladders and are holding less significant jobs than they had earlier in their careers. In the last twenty years, the twenty fastest-growing categories of new jobs paid wages that averaged $5000 less than the twenty occupations that were in steepest decline. When a steelworker or auto worker moves to a high-tech company, he or she generally loses about 40 percent of the previous annual wage. This has caused a shrinkage in America's middle class, and we estimate that in the last five years 8 million families descended from middle-class status. It is estimated that approximately one-fifth of the new jobs of the future will be provided by high-tech or some upper-level professions, leaving four-fifths of the jobs to come mainly from the service industries. Put another way, that means that out of twenty students in the classroom, only four are likely to end up having what we consider "successful careers."

Developed countries have found that as we "deskill" our jobs, job opportunities disappear in the new industries, as well as in the older "smokestack" industries. Many low-level jobs in high technology are less secure, pay less, and require less skill. Since it takes less skill to assemble a computer part than it does to make steel, entrepreneurs have found that computer manufacturing can be done at one-tenth or one-twentieth the price in Singapore, Taiwan, or South Korea. Consequently, a substantial number of jobs have left our shores over the last twenty years.

A human capital crisis has overtaken America. Structural unemployment grows. Forecasters in the 1980s anticipated that technological transformation and economic change would compel the average worker to change careers four or five times before retirement. But that assumed there was a job to train into. More often there is not.

For many, frustration grows as skills learned over a lifetime become obsolete. Most workers must adapt their knowledge and skills to new technological demands. The entire U.S. work force needs retraining on an average of every five years.

During the period from 1970 to 2000, one-fifth of college graduates took jobs that did not require a college degree.

- Twenty-five to 35 percent of recent college graduates are estimated to be underemployed.
- In the first decade of the twenty-first century, nearly half of those who go to work after graduation will not get the kind of job traditionally held by college graduates. During the 1990s there was a surplus of 200,000 to 300,000 graduates per year.
- Forty-three percent of college graduates over the last twenty years were not doing college-level work.
- Government, indirectly or directly, generated 50 percent of all jobs held by college graduates in the last twenty years, compared with only about one-third of all employment.
- During the 1980s and 1990s, college graduates were more likely to be working in a blue-collar or service job than they were in the 1970s.

Our society cannot productively put to use all those we graduate. Learning has to be its own reward, for often the economy doesn't reward the effort. It is no longer a ticket to a good job.

We have ceased trying to retrain the poor. We now buy them off with income maintenance. We call them "displaced workers" as if a job were imminent. But jobs are not imminent, and often workers are not prepared to train for those that are available. One-third of dislocated workers lack a high school diploma and another third have a high school diploma but are still functionally illiterate. The United States has "surplus people" — at least in an economic sense. These are people who are not prepared to function productively: they are either illiterate, unskilled, or have obsolete skills.

Tragically, the United States is moving toward a dual economy, where professionals, scientists, engineers, technicians, and other skilled employees are on one end of the spectrum and a large number of blue-collar workers, clerks, and service workers are on the other, with not much in between.

A trip through a modern office or factory demonstrates this convincingly. With the voice typewriter and other computerized equipment, most of the skilled secretaries and white-collar workers have been replaced by technology. There is much less need for supervisors. Only the computer operators, the computer service people, and the legal staff remain at full strength. In the factory, it is much the same scene. Robots and computers have eliminated and deskilled a massive number of jobs.

This administration has inherited rising long-run unemployment, a proliferation of low-wage jobs, and increasing economic dislocation. We must manage and try to eliminate a job drought inherited from our predecessors.

Memorandum

To: The President
From: The Chief of the Forest Service
Re: Requiem for the Forests
Date: January 20, 2001

When I was young, a popular children's book character called the Lorax asked, "Who will speak for the trees?"

This question has never been answered. As long as it remains unanswered, a tragedy that is already happening will continue to impoverish all inhabitants on earth. The world's forests are being destroyed much faster than they are being regenerated. Broad-scale conversions of tropical forests are occurring at such rapid rates that many countries have destroyed essentially all of their tropical forests. Scientists have estimated that the same fate will befall the world's remaining tropical forests by 2025. The tragedy is that much of the utilitarian, ecological, and aesthetic benefits of forests are being irretrievably lost to us before we even have a chance to understand the nature and magnitude of that loss.

The cedars of Lebanon, perhaps the world's most famous trees, once covered the higher slopes of mountains at the eastern end of the Mediterranean. The cedars provided a universal resource and were prized by all nations. They furnished the wood that built early civilizations. The Egyptians and Babylonians, the Syrians and Persians, and the Phoenicians all harvested vast quantities of these cedar trees for their ships. Even the Greek and Roman fleets and the interior of King Solomon's temple were made from these cedars. One poet called them "the most famous national monument in the universe," and added, "They know the history of the earth more than history itself. They could tell us, if they could speak, about many empires, religions and human races that have disappeared."

The insatiable demands finally overtook the finite supply of the cedars of Lebanon. After visiting the heavily cut cedar forests, the Roman emperor Hadrian enacted the first known forestry law by issuing an order prohibiting any further logging of the cedar forests. Unfortunately, his order was ignored by centuries of multiple civilizations. Today only a few trees remain, and much of the area once covered by these beautiful trees is now barren. The world has lost an irreplaceable resource.

Forests provide an invaluable renewable resource and a primary source of welfare for people everywhere, in ways they never suspect. Tropical forests, for example, cover a little more than 9 million square kilometers (only one-sixth of the earth's land surface) but they provide more than any other ecological zone of similar size. Forests provide a reservoir of genetic diversity and a vast supply of forest products. They help regenerate soils, maintain soil quality, and protect soils from erosional forces, thereby protecting watersheds and downstream areas from floods and siltation. They moderate climatic conditions and provide recreation and tourism.

There is no question that forests are important for industry and commerce. Forests provide food, medicines, pharmaceuticals, and industrial goods such as gums, resins, waxes, and rubber. About one out of four medicines or pharmaceuticals is derived directly or indirectly from raw materials from tropical forests, and at least 1400 species of tropical forest plants contain ingredients that are active against cancer. Coffee, a diversity of fruits and nuts, and chocolate all come from forests. American supermarkets receive two fruits from the forests of New Guinea, but there are 250 other species of edible-fruit-bearing trees from these same forests. Forests clearly contain an exceptional stock of natural resources for the future. As Norman Myers, an expert on tropical forests, has said, "If species can prove their worth through their contributions to agriculture, technology, and other down-to-earth activities, they can stake a strong claim to survival space in the crowded world."

Healthy, natural forest ecosystems maintain essential ecological processes and life-support systems, such as generating oxygen, recycling nutrients, breaking down pollutants, maintaining soil fertility, controlling water availability, and moderating climate. They also provide habitat for a diversity of species of plants and animals which contribute to the stability of the ecosystem in which they (and humans) live. Tropical forests, almost certainly the oldest continuous ecosystems on earth, alone provide habitat for 2 to 4 million of the earth's estimated 5 to 10 million living species. Their relatively stable climatic history has allowed evolution to be creatively diverse, resulting in an incredible biological diversity found nowhere else on the planet. The tropical forests in Ecuador contain several thousand more species of plants than in all of Europe, a land mass thirty-one times greater. Nearly 2600 species of birds are so restricted to forest habitats that if their forests were destroyed they would all be eliminated. And fifty different species of orchids have been found growing on one tree!

Forests have strong aesthetic values. Standing alone in the depth of a forest, one can feel the beauty, the power, and the natural vulnerability of the surrounding trees. Whereas humans in the temperate zones have historically feared the forests, alienated themselves from them, and tried to tame them by destroying them, humans in the tropics feel at one with the forests. As stated in "An Intro-

duction to the World Conservation Strategy": "The pres-
ervation of diversity is both a matter of insurance and
investment — necessary to sustain and improve agricultural, forestry and fisheries production, to keep open
future options, as a buffer against harmful environmental change, and as the raw material for much scientific and industrial innovation — and a matter of moral
principle."

It is all the more unfortunate, then, that the cedars of
Lebanon are a harbinger of what could happen — and what
is happening — to all of the world's forests. The U.S. Congress's Office of Technology Assessment has stated, "Each
year approximately 11.3 million hectares of the earth's remaining tropical forests — an area roughly the size of
Pennsylvania — are cleared and converted to other uses."
Every four days, we are destroying an area the size of New
York City. Where tropical forests worldwide once covered
about 16 million square kilometers, they now cover a little
over 9 million square kilometers. Already, Latin America
and Asia have each lost about two-fifths of their original
forests and Africa has lost over 50 percent. Today, very
little remains of all forests in Bangladesh, India, Sri Lanka,
Thailand, Vietnam, Central America, Madagascar, and
West Africa; of lowland forests in Australia, Indonesia,
Malaysia, Melanesia, the Philippines, Brazil, Colombia; and
of many of the forests in East Africa and Ecuador.

Unfortunately, the countries having the richest forests
are among the poorest in economic resources and in income. As these countries desperately try to rise out of poverty, they use their forests on a once-and-for-all basis.
Their people, caught up in day-to-day survival, are consuming today the capacity of the land to support them or
us tomorrow.

Forests are succumbing to three sets of different pressures. One is the desperate struggle of the poor people in

the Third World countries to stay alive and earn a living. Their demands for usable free land and for fuel wood have a major impact on forests. Since almost half of the population of the tropics is under sixteen, this impact will increase as the population grows. Small-scale, slash-and-burn farmers are clearing about 250,000 square kilometers of primary and secondary tropical forest per year. In the rural areas of the Third World countries, there are about 1.2 billion people who are essentially completely landless. These unecologically aware and hungry people follow existing roads to the fringes of the forests, cut trees, cultivate the marginal land by planting corn or other crops for a few years, and then cut further into the forest. Other desperate people plant on the already spent land, leaving no opportunity for the land to rejuvenate.

At least half of all wood cut around the world each year is burned as fuel. About four-fifths of that wood is cut in developing countries where more than 2 billion people rely on wood for fuel to cook meals. Although the primary impact is now on savannah woodlands, scrub forests, and local wood lots, there will be increasing pressure on forests. Today 2.3 billion people have trouble finding adequate fuel supplies and 350 million cannot even find wood for their minimal needs.

The second set of pressures on our forests is the excessive or carelessly applied commercial demand coming largely from people in developed countries. There are seemingly insatiable demands for wood, paper products, and inexpensive beef. Each American uses about two tons of wood per year and has a growing appetite. The global consumption of industrial wood has doubled since 1980 and will double again by 2025, with the developed countries consuming three-quarters. Hardwoods, occurring largely in the tropical forests of the world, are made into luxury items such as pleasure boats, stereo cabinets, and quality bedroom furniture. The United States imports a sizable portion of the current overharvest occurring in Southeast Asia, the region under the greatest pressure from exploitation.

The global demand for paper products is growing at twice the population growth. In only thirty years, demand has more than quadrupled, with an estimated 400 million tons today likely to double by 2020. The United States leads the pack, with each individual using about 300 kilograms per year compared to 150 kilograms per year per citizen in Great Britain or Japan. An average citizen in the developing countries annually uses paper in an amount equivalent to two copies of the Sunday edition of the *New York Times*.

The demand by the United States, Japan, and Western Europe for inexpensive (half the price of American beef), noninflationary beef for the fast-food trade has caused what Norman Myers calls the "hamburgerization" of the tropical forests in Central America. Every other meal eaten in the United States is purchased at a fast-food facility or at an institution (such as a hospital or school), and more than one-third are hamburgers.

The commercial demands for wood, paper, and beef are being met at the expense of the world's forests. Modern technology has provided a chipping machine that can reduce all of an average-sized tree of any species into chips the size of a silver dollar — in about one minute. In one working day, it can convert 12.5 acres of forest into chips for cardboard boxes and paper plates. As beef exports expand, two-thirds of Central America's virgin forests are already gone. In Latin America alone, ranchers are clearing about 20,000 square kilometers of tropical forests per year by felling and burning all of the trees.

The third type of pressure on forests was first noticed in 1979: airborne pollutants from electric utilities, industrial facilities, and motor vehicles. Pollutants such as sulfur oxide and nitrogen turn acidic in the moisture of the atmosphere. One theory about what may be happening is that doses of pollutants are altering one or more life-sustaining processes and causing tree death. Acid deposition may be triggering alterations in the soil environment that adversely affect a tree in various ways through its roots. For example, an uptake of excess nitrogen from the soil may be decreasing the ability of trees to seal their buds before frost, a natural form of frost resistance. Another theory is that high sulfur dioxide and ozone concentrations damage the cell membranes, inhibit the process of photosynthesis, and disturb the functions of the leaves and the internal flow of water.

Forests have never died so rapidly or so extensively as they have been dying recently in central Europe. In the Federal Republic of Germany, symptoms of forest decline such as yellowing, loss of needles, and death of new shoots were first observed in 1979. Data for 1984 state that 51.8 percent of all forests in West Germany showed symptoms of decline, and today 70 percent show symptoms of decline. Acid deposition may be having a negative effect on forest health and productivity in the eastern United States and in California. Scientists are researching the recent observations of forest decline in populations of red spruce and Fraser fir in the high-elevation forests of the northern and southern Appalachians, of lodgepole pine in California's San Bernardino Mountains, and of jack pines in California's Sequoia National Forest. On top of Mount Mitchell, the highest peak in eastern North America, over 40 percent of the red spruce trees are already dead. The affected forests are located above the cloud base for a large portion of the year and cloud moisture contains relatively high concentrations of pollutant substances.

There are no new worlds to colonize when a "timber famine" results from finite and vulnerable forests being overrun by our excessive demands and pollutants, and by exploding populations desperately looking for firewood and agricultural land. The consequences and potential catastrophes range from local and regional environmental damage to possible global climatic changes to the extinction of a major portion of the world's species during the lifetime of people now living.

The forests of Amazonia and of Southeast Asia are already so reduced that settlers and farmers are suffering floods and water shortages every year with an increasing intensity. The Ganges Plain, home to half a billion people, could well be the greatest single ecological hazard on earth. Forest cover upstream from the Ganges Plain in India and Nepal has decreased by 40 percent in the last thirty years. The 1978 monsoon rains rushed down the denuded slopes taking topsoil that burdened the upstream river channels with suspended sediments and flooding waters. In only a few weeks, 65,712 villages were inundated, forty thousand cattle were washed away, property damage exceeded $2 billion, and more than two thousand people drowned.

Denuded forest lands expose their soil to the sun, which bakes it into an unproductive crust, or to the rains, which wash it away. It is estimated that Nepal loses 30 to 75 tons of soil annually from each hectare (2.5 acres) of deforested land. Annual deposits of more than 1300 million cubic yards shorten the lives of major U.S. reservoirs. Watersheds of the Panama Canal have lost half their forest cover in less than thirty years. As the canal fills up with sediment, water supply, power production, and the ability of ships to pass through the canal could be drastically reduced.

Many once-vegetated areas are now deserts. Misery and dislocation caused by desertification are growing geometrically. The United Nations estimates that 36.3 percent of the earth's surface is extremely arid or semi-arid, conditions generally categorized as deserts. However, present soil and vegetation data identify 43 percent of the earth as desert. It is possible that this difference of 6.7 percent is newly manmade desert. The Agency for International Development estimates that 650,000 square kilometers of land once suitable for agriculture and intensive grazing have been forfeited to the southern edge of the Sahara Desert over the past fifty years. The spread of the Sahara is an ecological malignancy undermining the food-producing capacity of a vast area of Africa. Overgrazing, deforestation, and improper agricultural practices have also turned great stretches of Kenya, Tanzania, and Ethiopia into irreversible marginal land.

Burning of felled timber in the tropics could be releasing 4 to 8 billion tons of carbon dioxide into the atmosphere every year. Carbon dioxide is taken in from the air by living plants and returned to the atmosphere when plants decay or are burned. Since carbon dioxide absorbs some of the sun's energy and retains it at the earth's surface, increasing carbon dioxide could be warming the earth's atmosphere. A global warming could change the amount of rainfall, cloud cover, and wind, as well as the length of growing seasons and the height of sea level. These changes could alter crop yields, fish populations, and shipping routes, thus influencing national or individual wealth, shifting trade balances, and increasing or decreasing world hunger.

As our forests vanish, so do the teeming life forms that they support. As sociobiologist E. O. Wilson said, "The worst thing that can happen — *will* happen — is not energy depletion, economic collapse, limited nuclear war, or conquest by a totalitarian government. As terrible as these catastrophes would be for us, they can be repaired within a few generations. The one process ongoing in the last twenty years that will take millions of years to correct is the loss of genetic and species diversity by the destruction of natural habitats. This is the folly our descendants are least likely to forgive us." When a species is gone, it is gone forever.

A mega-extinction of species around the world is already occurring as a direct result of the destruction of the tropical forests where the greatest diversity of species live. These forests are so rich because, like the forests in Southeast Asia, some of them have evolved for more than 70 million years. Not all extinctions occur in the tropics, however. Logging probably caused the extinction of the ivory-billed woodpecker, which lived only in mature forests in the southern United States. Some scientists estimate that the current rate of extinction is 10,000 species a year, or one species every hour! If these pathetic rates continue, we could annihilate in our lifetimes a quarter of the species that now live on earth. This tragedy is compounded by the fact that only about a sixth of all species in the world have even been identified and named by scientists! In a real sense, we do not even know the magnitude of our loss because we are losing species we never even knew existed.

Measures to save the remaining primary (original, virgin) forests and to conserve the long-term sustainability of what is left of the world's secondary (already disturbed) forests will be expensive, difficult, and as challenging as any other resource issue confronting humankind. But it will be even more difficult to compensate for the harm done to society if the world's forests continue their rapid decline. As Sandra Postel, a resource analyst, has stated:

The biosphere is not infinitely resilient. What is happening in the industrial world's forests is a sign that fossil-fuel combustion has ecological limits and that exceeding them exacts a price. Unless energy and environmental strategies begin to reflect this, today's threats are bound to become tomorrow's catastrophes. The real test is whether nations so far spared severe losses will muster the political will to take action to avoid them. Nations can be confident that by encouraging energy efficiency, recycling, and renewable energy sources . . . they will help protect their forests, crops, lakes and people for generations. The connections are real, and so are the consequences of ignoring them.

Projections in this memo are based on the assumption that current rates of forest destruction will continue. Our challenge is to stop this destruction. There are numerous ways to improve on these rates. The people of the Third World are beginning to recognize that sustainable growth and economic development can occur on an ecologically sound basis. Development that does not give proper consideration to protecting and maintaining the natural resource base cannot be sustained over the long term. However, these countries just do not have the technical and financial resources to ensure wise use and management of their biological resources without the support and cooperation of the developed countries.

The world's remaining primary forests could be left intact if all forest goods and services were derived solely from the remaining secondary forests. Secondary forests have a more uniform structure as well as a higher percentage of fast-growing species, resulting in a more readily renewable resource. Better standards could be designed and implemented that would help ensure the maintenance of essential ecological processes such as watersheds, the protection of uncut trees from unnecessary damage, the planting of the same species that were cut, the inspection and control of logging operations by the governments in the countries where logging is occurring. Forests would benefit if people who require fuel wood had better stoves and also access to trees that are felled to make room for ranching, to charcoal made from the felled trees, or to local community tree lots.

Is the crisis with the world's forests not also a matter of excessive demand? Norman Myers, an expert on tropical forests, asks a good question: "Whose hand is on the chain saw at work in the tropical forests?" Putting the impact from local people aside for the moment, we must answer by saying that much of the excessive and destructive logging is conducted by giant timber corporations based in the United States, Western Europe, and Japan. These corporations are in business to fill our currently insatiable demands.

The current destruction of our forests is a short-term solution to the present level of demand. It is not only turning out to be counterproductive, it is also leading full tilt to a disaster. We must decrease our demands. We must adopt lifestyles that, when pursued over the long term, do not lead to catastrophes, but rather to a future that can be sustained by the resources of this planet. We are the ones who must speak for the trees!

Memorandum

To: The President
From: The Comptroller of the Currency
Re: A History of the Banking Crisis of 1991
Date: January 20, 2001

The important thing to remember about the banking crisis of 1991 is that it all started with responsible people acting in good faith to do their duty as they saw it. The crisis in banking was directly caused by the crisis of international debt, and the crisis of international debt was directly caused by the price of oil.

With OPEC organizing a successful increase in price in 1973, the price of petroleum quadrupled on the world markets. The OPEC nations, awash with cash, deposited those dollars in free world banks, which in turn lent much of the money to developing nations in Africa, Latin America, and Asia. This process was called "recycling." Then these non-oil-producing debtor countries ran up huge trade deficits because of the spiraling price of imported oil, and they could not pay their foreign debts. By 1984, the Third World was impossibly burdened with an $800 billion debt, which, essentially, it could not repay. By 1984, eight nations in Latin America alone owed approximately $300 billion, and their interest payments of $40 billion a year were equal to about two-fifths of their income from exports. Argentina and Brazil owed three and a half times the amount that they annually received from exports. By 1990, the Third World's indebtedness, combined with continued high interest rates caused by the U.S. deficit and the failure of U.S. banks appropriately to account for the defaulted payments, had caused a major financial crisis.

The amount of principal and interest owed by the developing countries simply put them on an economic treadmill, and for many countries the interest charges alone became an intolerable percentage of their export earnings.

The Third World countries had to borrow more and more money to pay interest on their loans, thereby increasing their indebtedness and their vulnerability. In June 1984, both Ecuador and Bolivia announced unilaterally that they were suspending payments on either part or all of the debt that they owed.

Then came the run on Continental Illinois, America's eighth largest bank. It lost $4 billion in deposits in three days, threatening the stability of the entire banking system of the United States. The Federal Deposit Insurance Corporation had to come in and guarantee the deposits and act as lender of last resort by lending the bank $4 billion. The government had no choice, in view of the stakes, other than to make the guarantees and preserve the banking system. The nine largest U.S. banks, which had capital of approximately $28 billion, had loaned the Third World countries over $64 billion — more than twice their total net worth. Default would have meant disaster for these nine financial giants.

We shouldn't have been surprised. It was myopia approaching stupidity that we had allowed them to borrow so much money in the first place. We kept deluding ourselves that "a country can't go broke," but now we know better. These debts, of course, and their non-repayment, caused, in early 1991, the first banking crisis in the United States since the 1930s and drove a number of our leading banks into insolvency. They had to be rescued by the Federal Reserve, as with the Continental Illinois bail-out by the FDIC. This "rescue" could only be done by running the printing presses, thus causing more inflation. It was a choice between evils. But it was the beginning of the great crisis in confidence that swept world banking.

Back in 1984, every percentage point of U.S. interest rate increase cost the Latin American countries $3 billion, and the interest payments alone of many of those debtors — including Brazil, Mexico, Argentina, Venezuela, Chile, Peru, and Colombia — consumed more than 40 percent of all of their export revenues. While they didn't pay us back, or even pay us very much on the interest, the International Monetary Fund imposed tough conditions on those countries. Between 1981 and 1983, Latin America reduced its imports, mostly from the United States, by $33.2 billion, or 41 percent, which resulted in a massive loss of U.S. jobs. The United States then ended up in the worst of all possible worlds — not getting its debts repaid, having to lend those countries money even to pay their interest, and losing a considerable amount of trade in the process.

From the present vantage point, we can see that it was impossible for the Third World debtors to regain the economic growth rates that they needed for political stability and still pay these large capital-exporting interest payments, let alone the capital, to the developed world's banks. No amount of Third World "austerity" was politically acceptable enough to begin to pay even the interest. A giant house of cards had been constructed.

One international finance expert, Lord Lever, summed it up: "Will it be politically feasible on a sustained basis for the governments of the debtor countries to enforce the measures that would be required to achieve even the payment of interest? Can it be seriously expected that hundreds of millions of the world's poorest populations would toil away in order to transfer resources to the international banks?"

It was the ultimate stupidity. We paid money, at exorbitant prices, for OPEC oil. OPEC countries turned around and put the money in our banks, and we lent it out to underdeveloped countries who then could not pay us back. This economic folly cost us a staggering amount of our national wealth.

The countries that we didn't lend money to, such as Taiwan, South Korea, Hong Kong, and Singapore, were the economic miracles of the 1970s and 1980s. Their governments stimulated growth by freeing the private sector from governmental controls and encouraging labor-intensive industries. They didn't borrow their wealth, they created it; and they increased both the public consumption and their private wealth and at the same time made more benefits available to their people than most socialist countries.

The countries that did borrow from the developed world increased their dependency and ended up not only hurting themselves but dramatically hurting their creditors when we had to inflate our money supply through the Federal Reserve to absorb the defaulted loans.

In the year 2000 we are thus again faced with the question of massive need in the Third World, but we must ask ourselves whether the industrialized free world realistically should continue to subsidize what the secretary of agriculture has called the "never-to-be-developed countries." Essentially, we are faced with the question, Should we support Third World countries that present us on the television news with appalling sights of riots, starvation, and social turmoil? But, realistically, once we start to support them, how would we ever be able to stop?

It is doubtful that loans made in the name of compassion win permanent friends or produce any long-run benefits for the United States. When we lend money to a Third World country, we may get a momentary wave of appreciation. But, at the opening of a new century, we must accept many Third World ills as chronic and incurable. American loans or aid are eventually taken for granted — and they do not help increase the capital wealth of the recipient nations. In effect, the people eat them and are hungry tomorrow. An honest Third World country that tries to pay its interest and reduce its debt may cause a poor people made poorer to take to the streets — and the honest government to be replaced by a regime that is not only in default but hostile toward its benefactor. It's thus that the quality of mercy is very greatly strained.

Forgotten Fundamentals of Public Policy: From a Speech by the Administrator of the Environmental Protection Agency to the National Education Association March 2000

Simply put, we forgot how much it costs to shoe a horse. I refer to the old high school mathematics riddle of the man who goes to a blacksmith to get his horse shod and asks, "How much?"

"One penny for the first nail," replies the blacksmith, "double the penny for the second nail, double that for the third, and so on."

"Cheap," says the man. "Go ahead!"

You will remember that the total is more money than there is in the whole town and the man loses his horse.

More dramatic is the story of the mathematician who sought his reward from the king for a favor owed by requesting that the King "merely" double a single grain of wheat on a chessboard for all the squares on the board. We learned that the last square on the board took 2^{63} grains and that the total wheat would be more than all the wheat *ever* harvested in all of human history.

We are in trouble today because we ignored the geometry of public policy.

We do not recognize how fast our world is being transformed. The number of changes is exponential and startling. They signal dramatic and traumatic alteration for our society. We are seeing a decade of change every year.

Whatever the numbers of each particular problem — which are impressive enough standing alone — we must recognize that we are seeing them all unfold simultaneously. We live in a period of convergence, and our survival depends upon our ability to recognize the geometry of public policy.

I believe that one of our basic and most common problems is our failure to understand the complications caused by geometric growth. We thus miss the cause and identify only the symptoms. It's like an individual who eats some mushrooms and is poisoned by them. The doctor gives him an emetic and cures him. He goes to the cook who prepared the mushrooms and says to him, "The mushrooms in white sauce made me ill yesterday! Tomorrow you must prepare them with brown sauce." Our individual eats the mushrooms in brown sauce. Second poisoning, second visit of the doctor, and second cure by the emetic.

"By Jove!" says he, to the cook, "I want no more mushrooms with brown or white sauce. Tomorrow you must fry them." Third poisoning, with accompaniment of doctor and emetic.

"This time," cries our friend, "they shall not catch me

again! . . . Tomorrow you must preserve them in sugar."
The preserved mushrooms poison him again.

But that man is an imbecile, you say. Why does he not
throw away his mushrooms and stop eating them? Be less
severe, I beg you, because that imbecile is yourself; it is
ourselves; it is all humanity.

We must start to recognize the iron laws of geometric
growth. Tiny growth rates yield gargantuan consequences.
A 1000-year supply of any mineral or energy source at its
current level of consumption shrinks to a 104-year supply
at a moderate 3.5 percent annual growth rate in use, while
a 10,000-year supply would last only 170 years at a 3.5
percent growth rate.

We are living at the upper end of some disastrous growth
curves, and we had better understand their implications.
One dollar, at an interest rate of 5 percent per year compounded, will grow in 500 years to $72 billion and would
yield interest today at a rate of $114 per second. If left
untouched for another doubling time of 14 years, the account balance would be $144 billion and interest would be
accumulating at a rate of $228 per second. Similar dynam-
ics in public policy cause a torrent of change in the modern
world.

There are triple the number of people in the world as
there were on the day Lindbergh flew across the Atlantic;
triple the number of people in the United States as on the
day FDR was elected; triple the number of cars on the road
as when JFK was assassinated. Our health care costs are 50
percent higher than they were on that day in January 1997
when President Hesperus was sworn into office.

We are told that with the explosion of family planning
the world population growth rate was down to 1.64 percent
by 1999. What does that really mean? That means the next
billion people will be added to the world in 13.6 years
instead of 11.7.

Our average monthly salary this year, $20,000 per month, would have seemed unthinkable, even unimaginable, back in 1985. Yet in that year the United States had an inflation rate of 6 percent. Inflation of 6 percent will increase prices by a factor of 64 over seventy years. Bread to feed children, which costs 60 cents a loaf, will, at a 6 percent inflation rate, cost $38.40 when those children retire seventy years later.

We can also see the effect of a 7 percent growth rate in electrical consumption and petroleum use that this country experienced in the 1950s and 1960s. When consumption grows at 7 percent per year, consumption in any decade is approximately equal to total consumption in *all of previous history*. At 7 percent a year growth, we consumed more petroleum in the 1950s than we had since 1859, when the first mechanically drilled oil well was dug in Titusville, Pennsylvania; and then, as 7 percent growth continued in the 1960s, we consumed more oil than in all history, including the 1950s.

Thus a new, important truth we have discovered far too late: when dealing with a steady growth over a long period we do not need to have an accurate estimate of the size of a resource in order to make a reliable estimate of the life expectancy of the resource.

One of the causes for the massive starvation of today is that we did not recognize (1) the new equation of agriculture, which is to use land merely as a place where we turn petroleum into food; and (2) how rapidly a 7 percent growth rate eats into existing petroleum stores.

Think for a moment of the effect of petroleum on American life. Petroleum has made it possible for American farms to be operated by a tiny fraction of our population: only one in thirty Americans now lives on a farm. The people thus displaced from our farms by petroleum-based mechanization have migrated to the cities, where our ways of life are virtually regulated by the availability of petroleum. Without the people to do the work, farms are critically dependent on petroleum-based mechanization. The approaching exhaustion of domestic reserves of petroleum and the rapid depletion of world reserves will have a profound effect on Americans in the cities and on the farms. It is clear that agriculture as we know it has experienced major changes within the life expectancy of most of us, and these changes have caused a major further deterioration of worldwide levels of nutrition. The doubling time of world population, either every thirty-six years at a 1.9 percent growth rate, or every forty-two years at 1.64 percent, means that we have this period of time in which to double world food production — that is, if we wish to do no better than hold constant the fraction of the world population that is starving. This would mean that the number starving at the end of the doubling time would be *twice* the number that are starving today.

We were warned. For example, Robert O. Anderson, chairman of Atlantic Richfield, stated in 1979: "There is every likelihood that the world has reached the practical limits of oil production. We can expect the decline in production to begin in the next couple of years."

Curves can be changed. Extrapolations of trends are hazardous because the dynamics of world affairs are always changing, and trends are not destiny. I recognize this. But the forgotten fundamental of public policy is how fast the geometry of public policy expands a problem. Problems in the twenty-first century will come at us faster and with more momentum than at any time in human history.

That is the forgotten fundamental of public policy.

PART TWO

Copernican Politics

If we are to arrive at the year 2000 and view about us a world worth living in and worth turning over to future generations, we must conceive most of that world today and build it with every succeeding tomorrow.

— Glenn T. Seaborg

The Morgenstern Years

The following pages are an excerpt from *America in the Twentieth Century: A History of the Past Hundred Years,* by Cornelius Barnes. Boston: Houghton Mifflin Company, 2010.

"Headline writers," wrote Sir John Squire (in the introduction to his 1931 book *If It Had Happened Otherwise*), "are fond of citing 'The Parting of the Ways.' But every moment we are at the parting of the ways. There is no action or event, great or small, which might not have happened differently and, happening differently, have perhaps modified the world's history for all time. Carlyle said that an Indian on the shores of Lake Ontario could not throw a pebble a few yards without altering the globe's centre of gravity. By the same token, if that Indian should occupy his time in some other manner — such as composing a war song which might later infuriate a tribe to attack, or killing a settler whose vote might have turned an election — it is evident that these deeds would send ripples of action out to change the course of the world . . . Though history be, as Gibbon remarked, 'a record of the crimes and follies of mankind,' we do sometimes think that if something had happened differently, things might have turned out far better or worse."

What "happened differently" in the year 1991 was the unexpected rise to national prominence of a little-known Maine senator named Martin Morgenstern.

After the aimless drift of the second Reagan administration and the near-disaster of the Bush administration, America was at a very low point in her fortunes. She was ready to accept a forceful leader with a new vision of the future. It was then that Morgenstern appeared.

The Second New Deal

The turning point in the second half of the twentieth century was clearly the election in 1992 of President Martin Morgenstern.

A great deal has been written about what is variously called the American Renewal or the Breakthrough Years. I prefer to call it the American Renewal, because while it was a significant breakthrough reminiscent of the New Deal, it was less than a revolution. Alexis de Tocqueville, commenting almost two hundred years ago on the stability of American opinion, said that in a democracy "the public is engaged in infinitely varying the consequences of known principles . . . rather than in seeking for new principles," and "thus democratic nations have neither time nor taste to go in search of novel opinions." The core values sustain a society, and stability rather than revolution is the norm. When change does take place, it usually does so by reapplication of old values and institutions rather than by revolution. Revolution is history's last gasp of a society that doesn't reform itself.

Morgenstern was a morale and confidence builder whose motto was, "You can do very little with faith, but you can do nothing without it." He believed in what he was doing and he had the power to convince others. He was a man of thought and action. On his wall he hung a sign that read, "Difficulty is the one excuse that history never accepts."

John Gardner cites Jean Monnet, father of the Common Market, and Morgenstern as modern leaders who outclassed Charles de Gaulle. Both, he said, had the patience to work in a context of complexity and pluralism; the intellectual clarity to conceptualize a workable consensus; the flexibility to revise their conception; the integrity to win the trust of contending forces; and the persuasiveness to mobilize a constituency of willing allies in pursuit of goals that are tolerable for all. But Morgenstern had an additional trait, a sense of the future, and he had a crisis to galvanize action.

The Morgenstern years, for all the change, were years of reform, not violence. The tumultuous times of the early 1990s seemed ripe for a populist revolution, but, most fortunately, they produced a George Washington kind of leader rather than a Samuel Adams kind, and America was saved by the inherent stability of democracy that Tocqueville found so impressive.

Morgenstern's leadership exemplified President Harry Truman's definition: "You know what makes leadership? It is the ability to get men to do what they don't want to do and like it." That would seem to describe Morgenstern's style and summarize his accomplishments. Morgenstern, like Churchill, could ask the people of a democracy for sacrifice and make them recognize it was necessary. Left by President Bush with a deficit-burdened nation whose economy was shattered, Morgenstern took bold and decisive action immediately after his inauguration in 1993.

But that in itself is insufficient. In the preceding decades,

Lyndon Johnson had been a "bold and decisive" leader who couldn't win either a war on poverty or a war in Vietnam. Gerald Ford was bold and decisive in the *Mayaguez* incident, but he landed the Marines on the wrong island. Richard Nixon "dynamically" ordered American troops into Cambodia, and Ronald Reagan's "boldness" led him to double the deficit in eight years.

The best description of Morgenstern's style comes from John Morley's *Life of Richard Cobden.* "Great economic and social forces flow with a tidal sweep over communities that are only half conscious of that which is befalling them. Wise statesmen are those who foresee what time is thus bringing and endeavor to shape institutions and to mold men's thought and purpose in accordance with the change that is silently surrounding them."

Leadership is a matter of asking anew the big questions of the world and — in place of worn-out formulas — supplying answers that work better than the old ones. When Copernicus said to himself, "Perhaps, instead of the sun going around the earth, the earth goes around the sun," he asked the right question and prepared the way for a revolutionary answer. The 1990s were surely a Copernican era in the history of the United States.

Most historians have attributed Morgenstern's success to his personal leadership and his peculiar ability to get Americans to make hard choices. Not many of them realize that his genius — shared by the brilliant members of the Cabinet he assembled — was to ask precisely the right questions, based on the right premises, and to see the better answers (for there are no absolute answers, just worse or better ones).

His greatest achievement was to understand the implications of a simple truth: the world grows smaller and poorer day by day. Just as before Copernicus the sun had always been observed circling the earth, in the four centuries of American history, the world grew steadily larger and richer. Energy sources grew from muscle and wind to steam to electricity to oil and finally to nuclear power. Available land grew from a thin thirteen-colony strip of shoreline to vast continental stretches. Technology grew from a wooden wagon to a jet airplane. All of this combined to be the shaping force of the American mind. But sometime in the eighth decade of the twentieth century, the forces of history took a deep geological shift and all the world of great expectations became obsolete.

The place was getting smaller. The ground was getting worn out and used up. Your neighbors were crowding your space — because there were two and a half billion more of them than there were when you were born. The accepted policy of caring for and supporting every human being in the land from infancy through senility was growing too much for a smaller work force to pay for. The nation's debt was becoming both a fantasy that could never be controlled and a poison that debilitated the whole economic system.

Clear as this has become since, it was hard to recognize in the early years of the 1980s. There were some Cassandra prophets who were much derided as doomsayers. They tried to explain that the luxurious years when everything was expendable and quickly replaceable were past. They tried to explain that certain social policies that began as humane and decent undertakings had, finally, ended as intolerable burdens on the people of the country. Such warnings were ignored. It took the economic crash of 1991 to make the public aware that the old answers no longer served. The next year, Morgenstern was elected — out of a sense more of desperation than of confidence.

If our age's turning point can be fixed to any moment in time, it must be to the hour of the new President's inaugural address. It was undoubtedly the most extraordinary inaugural speech in the history of the republic, because it made some very deadly assumptions about the nature of reality in 1993. There was snow on the streets of Washington and the air was icy when the new President began to speak. When he finished — as a witticism of the time put it — the town was a glacier.

Morgenstern's message was generally oversimplified by the press in the following days. At least one of his homely sayings made for arresting headlines: he cited the old New England adage "Use it up, wear it out; make it do, or do without." He added, "The future belongs to the educated and to the efficient." At a glance, it seemed that he was offering a kind of Poor Richard philosophy to a very troubled nation. Actually, as his governmental strategy began to unfold in the following weeks, it became clear that what he was offering was a very sophisticated set of assumptions about the dismal state of the nation and about the future. "Beware of solutions appropriate to the past but disastrous to the future," he said. The assumptions on which the United States had been making plans for forty years — those assumptions that had become part of the vested interests of government, business, and individuals — were now wrong. The new set of premises was based on the concept that the United States was part of a contracting world. The new answers would have to form a strategy of providence, economy, efficient effort, and guardianship of a common wealth whose limits were now known.

In the catch phrase of the time, the country had before it a "static economic pie." In the 1970s and 1980s, the economy had slowed, faltered, and then slid back. Median family income in 1970 was $20,939, and by 1980 it had risen by only $84. Inflation, however, had wiped out all increases in wages and benefits. Things were better in

1984, as the inflation rate dropped and wages and benefits rose, but, again, these gains were wiped out by the recession of the late 1980s. It was beginning to be apparent that there would be higher swings and lower swings but that the era of sustained growth of 5 percent over each decade was unlikely to occur again. No economy in the history of the world had maintained that rate for long.

America had done it because she had been blessed by fortune with a virtually empty continent, rich in natural resources — which included some of the best topsoil in the world. The swiftness of the reversal was bewildering: the stage had been set for a new leader.

Economic Dunkirk

Much has been written about Morgenstern's "sense of the future." He clearly was what C. G. Jung called an "extroverted intuitive," which gave him an uncanny insight and feeling for where society was going. "He was always two steps ahead of us," said one of his Cabinet officers. "He could sense the future and how he could use it to instill hope rather than despair."

That ability to seize the day — not the present day, but tomorrow — and to make the right decisions about events that had not yet occurred was aptly described by Bismarck when he observed, "Political genius consists of hearing the distant hoofbeats of the horse of history and leaping to catch the passing horseman by the coattails. The difficulty is that one may hear the wrong horse or lunge for the horseman."

Without the banking crisis of 1991 it is doubtful that Morgenstern could have risen to power.

An economic Dunkirk was as necessary to the emergence

of Morgenstern as the military Dunkirk was to that of Churchill in 1940. "Reality therapy," Morgenstern called the banking crisis. In his first-term acceptance speech at the Democratic Convention in Chicago in 1992, he stated:

> Ronald Reagan told us that America was eternal. Only a person ignorant of history could have said that. No civilization has ever been eternal or could ever be eternal. Show me a self-satisfied civilization and I'll show you a civilization heading for a fall.
>
> Civilizations are not static. They advance, then decline, and all civilizations eventually disintegrate. America must never think of itself as eternal or we shall fall into complacency. The wolves of history wait to cull out those civilizations that falter. America has no guarantee other than its own self-discipline, patriotism, and hard work. The hungry lion hunts best.

That was both compelling and a bit arrogant. The nation had to think back to the first inauguration of Franklin D. Roosevelt to find a comparison — a forceful leader who announced at once that he was going to lead. Roosevelt believed that the President should be the idea maker and pacesetter for the country. He said, "All our great Presidents were leaders of thought at times when certain historic ideas in the life of the nation had to be clarified. That is what the office is — a superb oportunity for . . . applying in new conditions the simple rules of human conduct to which we always go back."

Events made for an even closer parallel between FDR and the newly elected Morgenstern — each faced an economic crisis of enormous proportions when taking office. The banking crisis of 1991 helped to make Morgenstern's election possible, while Roosevelt's first test was the near-breakdown of the American banking system in March 1933.

At that time, with thousands of banks about to become insolvent, Roosevelt called a four-day bank holiday and got emergency legislation to allow the Federal Reserve System and the Reconstruction Finance Corporation to save the salvageable banks. Permanent corrective legislation followed, and the system was back in balance.

Morgenstern, however, was looking at a crisis on an even broader scale than the depression of the 1930s. Roosevelt had one great power in reserve — the national debt was only about $16 billion. There was a lot of equity to borrow on. Further, while Roosevelt could apply some quick-fix legislation (such as the Glass-Steagall Banking Act and the Securities Exchange Act), Morgenstern had to deal with a bigger and more complicated economy in serious trouble.

Crisis can get a nation a dictator as easily as a democratic leader. The depression of the 1930s spawned a Hitler in one country and a Roosevelt in another. America had the extraordinary good luck to have a democratic leader available in its two severest tests of the twentieth century. It could have gone the other way. In the 1930s a Huey Long and in the 1980s a Jesse Helms could have taken the nation in an opposite direction. Both had the potential, both led powerful forces, but both in the end fell short of taking power. One explanation is the divine-intervention theory ("God watches over drunks, fools, and the United States of America"), but a sounder view is that finding leadership in a crisis is the Russian roulette of history. There is no predicting what type of leader may arise once a crisis emerges. Hungry or desperate people are not choosy. They will gravitate to the leader who will solve their need, whatever the leader's morality. "First comes the belly, then morality," notes Bertolt Brecht in *The Threepenny Opera*.

In the latter half of the 1980s, neither the Reagan nor the Bush administration did much to educate the public about the worsening economic circumstances. By 1984, the federal government was borrowing 20 cents for every dollar it spent, and the interest on the national debt alone was more than $460 million a day. It was an example of a problem so big, so incomprehensible, and so ever-present that there was no longer energy to attack it. The nation was like a cancer patient who had resigned himself to living with his tumor.

There is no example in history of a people effecting — through popular force and popular demand — the curative self-sacrifice to correct a runaway economy. Candidates complain and then, becoming officeholders, transform themselves into part of the problem. One person would abolish a certain tax loophole, but to many of his neighbors it is a cherished tax incentive. Another considers his monthly government check simply a matter of social justice, while his cousin thinks that it is an example of welfare-state waste. This was precisely the situation in the United States in the 1980s. It was a problem that was psychologically impossible for the nation to solve. Toward the end of the decade, it became a crisis.

Russia in 1917, Germany in 1936, and China in 1949 solved such crises by letting power slip into the hands of gunmen. What a sick America did was, in effect, to find a surgeon. Morgenstern's success in dealing with the budget deficits, in stopping the hemorrhage of the trade deficit, and in restoring confidence in the national economy amounted to a severe and painful operation. But, in the twenty-first century, the patient is alive and well!

The Economy

President Morgenstern's first public policy goal of economic revitalization was clearly outlined from the beginning of his term. He said:

> The United States' economy is no longer supreme. We do not have a divine guarantee of prosperity. Nations remain wealthy only as long as their citizens work and as innovation creates new wealth. We must now accept the fact that our economic problems are not a series of recessions but the result of a long-term dry rot in our economy that has reduced productivity, capital reinvestment, exports, and innovation. Our economy will not fully recover without sacrifice by all of us.

His first task was to balance the federal budget and bring interest rates down. "There is no industrial policy that would be better than low interest rates," he told Congress in his first State of the Union Message. He pressed for a bipartisan effort to balance the budget by the formula "Raise a dollar, cut a dollar." He pressed Democrats to accept spending reductions and Republicans to accept tax increases. In this he had the powerful backing of a nonpartisan group of businessmen, former Presidents, and civic leaders who endorsed his program the day after the State of the Union Message. Congress was visibly impressed. The great majority of the members found the program simple, understandable, and effective.

The Federal Deficit

Morgenstern asserted that the United States had a "structural" federal deficit. "We cannot grow our way out of our current deficit any more than we can borrow our way to prosperity. We need fundamental changes in our systems — macro adjustments, not minor changes. There are no chocolate sundae diets."

The background was this: In fiscal 1981, when President Reagan took office, the federal budget was 21.1 percent of the gross national product. In fiscal 1984, federal spending would total more than 24 percent of the GNP, the highest percentage since World War II. The Reagan administration added $735 billion to the federal deficit in its first four years. In the eight years following 1984 — despite the tax increases in the latter part of the Reagan administration — another crushing $610 billion was added to the national debt. In 1970, the entire federal budget was $200 billion and the nation had, in that year, a $2.8 billion deficit. In 1983, the federal yearly budget exceeded $800 billion and the United States had a one-year deficit of about $200 billion. The deficit that year *exceeded* the total amount of money spent by the United States just thirteen years before. The federal deficit had grown from approximately 0.5 percent of the GNP to approximately 6 percent of the GNP, which was more than America saved. The interest alone spent to service the federal deficit exceeded the total amount of money that Lyndon Johnson spent to run the war on poverty, the Great Society, and the Vietnam War. The government's debt service costs, which were $23 billion in 1975, rose to $105 billion in 1984 and to approximately $198 billion in 1989. They grew and compounded. "It is a problem that, unless we have the discipline and the courage to solve it, will cause immense economic traumas to our society," Morgenstern said, adding, "America has to work incredibly hard if our children are to have an acceptable future."

In his famous Madison Square Garden campaign speech, Morgenstern went on to say:

Smokestack America is nearly bankrupt. And what do we make now instead of steel girders and heavy machinery? We make plastic amusement gadgets, and wearables (not clothes — those all come from Korea and Italy), and gift items, and tissue paper. Heavy industry finds it hard to borrow money to build the computer-run, robotized plants we need in order to compete with the rest of the world. Long-term borrowing at the prevailing high interest rates simply means disaster for such companies. Result? American industry can still supply a ten-cent store. But it's fast losing the capacity to build a shipyard or a steel mill.

Almost miraculously, that nationwide telecast of October 1992 cut through the national complacency as had no political speech in years. The nation, increasingly queasy and ill, had listened to Dr. Feelgood for years. Now, as the pains were getting sharp, it was ready to listen to Dr. Bitter Cure. The media reacted with overwhelming assent. Opinion polls showed that the speech had gathered the highest approval rating in recent years (82 percent positive as compared with President Bush's 27 percent positive rating at the time). The little-known senator from Maine proved that his intense and eloquent style could move many people, even when the message was like Cassandra's.

It showed up a deep division in the Republican party as well. The President's comment that "it's the same old gloom and doom we've been hearing from the Democrats for years" was hardly taken seriously. A few days later, on *Meet the Press,* Herbert Stein, chairman of the Council of Economic Advisers under Nixon, startled his listeners by endorsing Morgenstern's ideas. Even more surprising was Stein's statement that he was speaking on behalf of former Presidents Nixon and Ford. They both agreed, he said, that the deficit was a fiscal iceberg, and all of us were passengers aboard a *Titanic.* We had to correct course. We had to end the disaster of the high interest rates that were denying us any chance for recovery, and of the overvalued dollar that had almost ruined American export.

Morgenstern urged a solution of "shared sacrifice," including numerous budget cuts and tax increases, but his main thrust was in "means testing" entitlements. His call for "belt tightening for the sake of our children" was both inspirational and effective.

The Trade Deficit

Morgenstern challenged America to balance not only its federal deficit but its trade deficits. He charged that these deficits represented the export of America's wealth. In his first State of the Union Message, he said:

> In the last ten years, the United States has bought $650 billion more in goods from abroad than we have sold abroad. During this time, America's share of world sales declined by 30 percent while other nations increased their share. U.S. share of world automobile sales has declined by one-third, industrial machines by one-third, agricultural machinery by 40 percent, telecommunications equipment by 50 percent, metalworking machines by 50 percent. Overall, the value of manufacturing imports is growing twice as fast as the value of exports of American-made goods. Such figures do not bode well for the United States. They constitute a roadmap to bankruptcy.

The United States' trade position in the 1980s was largely dependent upon six key industries: aerospace, agriculture, chemicals, earthmoving equipment, computers, and machine tools. Historically, the United States had been the leader in every one of these industries. By 1984 the United States led in only two (aerospace and agriculture), and some 70 percent of our products faced intense foreign competition. The collapse of exports in the United States made the 1982–83 recession far worse and cost what economists estimate to be two million jobs. The economic cancer metastasized during the remainder of the decade.

Employment in textiles fell 3.5 percent a year in the 1980s. The metal industry has seen employment drop at an annual rate of 4.2 percent over a similar time span. The auto industry's work force had been falling at a rate of 3.1 percent since 1974. The lumber and wood-products industry had a steady erosion of 2.3 percent yearly during the same period. America was in liquidation.

Morgenstern said that he had developed a form of "reality therapy" for the American public: "America, for a long time you have been the victim of an insidious disease. It is a disease called illusions, and you scarcely suffered from its effects before you nearly died of them. Reality therapy is about to cure you."

The new President went on to say:

If you manufacture something in the United States today, you will discover some interesting problems about marketing. It's possible that no one in Denmark or Brazil will buy it because there are cheaper Japanese or German models of the same thing available. So that leaves Indianapolis, San Diego, and the rest of that rich continental market to sell it in? Not quite. A lot of that market is gone, too. Because in Indianapolis and San Diego, you are up against the same lower-priced foreign product. And, after your business has gone broke, your workmen have registered for unemployment compensation, and you have retired on Social Security, you read the latest economic survey. It shows conclusively that the value of manufactured imports is growing twice as fast as that of American-made exports. You are reading your own obituary.

Taxes

No sustained economic recovery was possible without a balanced budget, and spending cuts alone would not be sufficient to balance it. The numbers were simply too large. Taxes would have to be raised. Such a task has ended many a political career.

President Morgenstern recognized that he must reform and simplify the tax code before he raised taxes. The American public had grown cynical about a tax code that allowed one dollar in three to escape taxation and resentful of a tax code that allowed half a trillion dollars in "tax expenditures." Simply put, the American public, for very valid reasons, had lost confidence in the tax code.

The battle to simplify turned out to be harder than the battle to raise taxes. Every special interest descended on Congress to preserve their loopholes, and hundreds of millions of dollars went into lobbyists' pockets. In the end, a coalition of Congress members from both parties prevailed, with the help of Morgenstern, by taking their case directly to the American public. Showing example after example of unequal and unfair taxation, they built a "constituency for fairness" that demanded that "equal income be equally taxed." By offering people a tax system that was fair, they didn't eliminate the pain of paying taxes but they did instill a confidence that all were equally burdened. Americans did not like paying taxes, but they hated to the point of rebellion the inequity of the old system. Most were willing to pay some additional taxes if the money would go to reduce the deficit and would not be spent on new programs.

This accomplished, Morgenstern still had to raise taxes to balance the budget and reinstill confidence in the economy. His choice of method was quintessential Morgenstern: raising the gasoline and diesel tax.

"Petroleum is a finite resource and we should use the marketplace to encourage conservation," he declared. "America has been profligate in the use of this diminishing resource. Our fuel is far cheaper than in other industrialized countries, and our gasoline taxes are lower. Adam Smith's invisible hand is the best conservation method. The United States is far too wasteful of petroleum. We had better conserve now so that our children will have some remaining for their use."

Morgenstern proposed and Congress authorized a 40 cents per gallon tax on both gasoline and diesel fuel. America in 1992 was consuming 100 billion gallons of gasoline a year and 40 billion gallons of diesel. The new tax thus raised approximately $50 billion and completed Morgenstern's budget balancing, allowing him toward the end of his first term to start to amortize the national debt.

The gasoline and diesel tax thus helped three problems simultaneously: it raised revenue; it encouraged conservation; and, by decreasing the use of petroleum, it helped balance the foreign trade budget. Petroleum imports accounted for more than half the U.S. trade deficit and the reduction in use directly reduced the trade deficit. While not mentioned at the time, the gasoline and diesel tax also stimulated research into alternatives to petroleum use and thus called on one of America's basic strengths: creativity and innovation.

Morgenstern stated, "Taxes are the price we pay for national recovery and economic stability. We have matched the new taxes with equivalent spending cuts. Everyone can feel confident that the tax burden and spending burden are shared equally. It is painful but it is necessary to U.S. economic stability. We used our national credit card too long and now we must have the backbone to pay our bills."

Entitlements

One of the major problems facing the United States in the 1980s was that of entitlements — especially the Social Security system, which accounted for the major portion by far. Fortunately for the budget — and for the country — a bipartisan agreement between Congress and the Reagan administration back in 1983 had solved the problem until the end of the century. The rise in FICA taxes in the first years of the decade, a modest means test (for retirees, income over $25,000 became taxable), a gradual increase in the retirement age, and a more favorable ratio of workers to retirees (as a result of the baby boom generation entering the work force) all resulted in a small credit balance for Social Security after the fiscal year 1983.

Even though the problem had been sharply reduced by this, Morgenstern still was dismayed by the upward curve of military pensions, Veterans Administration hospital costs, Medicare, and other programs. He noted as particularly unfair the practice of "double dipping" or "triple dipping," which was engaged in by about 80 percent of federal government retirees — both civilian and military. The Barker-Croft Act of 1993 — legislation requiring each retiree to choose a "primary" pension and undergo a means test for any others — was bitterly fought in the Congress. Certain critics in the media even suggested that opposition resulted from the fact that many congressmen looked forward to excellent military pensions, congressional pensions, and, in some cases, private business pensions as well.

When that battle was won, however, it became easier for the Morgenstern administration to introduce modest means tests into most entitlement programs. The "indexing" of Social Security benefits was reduced. Thus, the poor were provided for as before, at no cost; the well-to-do were taxed moderately according to their means; and the rich were discouraged, by new and higher tax rates, from accepting federal entitlement benefits.

Means Testing

By far the most controversial part of Morgenstern's economic revitalization program was not the reduction of defense spending or the raising of taxes but his proposal to means-test all entitlements. Simply put, this meant that every person who got some sort of financial help from the government — whether in the form of a pension, agricultural payments, or anything else — had to be genuinely in need. Those who had the means to support themselves without federal help would have to be cut off the rolls.

When Morgenstern insisted on making this a plank in the party platform of 1992, the onslaught, predictably, came almost at once. He wanted to rob the man who had worked hard for his retirement pension; he wanted to beggar the middle classes; he meant to starve the elderly — all of this by abolishing entitlements and sustituting a charity dole.

These accusations he answered with great dignity and persuasiveness in his famous appearance before the annual meeting of the American Association of Retired Persons in September of that year. He said that it was impossible to balance the federal budget without touching entitlements. This was overwhelming fact number one. The next important fact was that up to now only a few of those individuals who got government checks (recipients in 13 percent of government programs) had to prove actual need.

He went on to say:

I am not here to accuse anyone of cheating or chiseling because he has accepted a government check. I'm here to ask for a patriotic sacrifice from people who are well enough off to make it. All of you have helped to build America. Many of you fought to protect her in one or more wars. Now, I am calling on you one more time — to save her from economic death.

This is the program I propose, put very simply: People who have adequate incomes should forgo Social Security and Medicare benefits. People who have pensions from several sources — military, civil service, and private business, for example — should make do with one. Wealthy land developers should no longer be given farm supports. No farmer who raises a product that is verifiably injurious to the health of the consumer should be given a price support. In short, we must forget the word *entitlements* as we used to understand it. Now it should mean just that our poor and helpless people will be taken care of, as always, through government aid. The rest of us will have to do what our grandfathers and grandmothers did — stand on our own feet. What is the great thing that we are now entitled to? To live in a country that is no longer in danger of destruction through impossible fiscal policies.

The program promised a balanced federal budget by three major thrusts: reduction of the rate of increase in defense spending; means-testing of entitlements and various other budget cuts; and tax increases.

The implementation of this program, long thought politically impossible, caused an immediate lowering of the interest rate and a healthy rally of the financial markets.

It remained for Morgenstern to start on his second "politically impossible" step: to reform America's health care system, which by 1989 was taking 20 cents of every dollar spent in America.

The Health Care Revolution

Morgenstern's ability to clarify and articulate political dilemmas was demonstrated in his groundbreaking speech to the American Medical Association in June 1993. He began with a challenge: "We shall continue to have a sick economy unless we control health care costs. We cannot spend on health to the exclusion of the other important needs of a society." He went on to announce that he was about to freeze the amount of federal money going into health care, and he challenged the health care delivery system to manage itself more efficiently. "In our budget there is more than enough money to keep America healthy. You have had the power to make your patients healthy at a cost that has made America economically sick. You must help our economy recover with the same dedication with which you serve your patients."

His speech is worth quoting in more detail:

> The most important reality to accept here is that we can't go on allocating increasing percentages of GNP to health care.
>
> America has some neglected societal values in which it must now invest. We have roads to build, infrastructure to repair, education systems to rejuvenate. We must retool and re-industrialize America.
>
> Health care costs are eroding our goals in the international marketplace and reducing our ability to compete with foreign companies. As Joseph Califano, Jr., then a Chrysler trustee, warned back in 1984, "Chrysler's health care costs will exceed $400 million, making the Blues [Blue Cross and Blue Shield] Chrysler's single largest supplier. That's more than $1.1 million each day. This year Chrysler must sell about seventy thousand vehicles just to pay for its health care bills."

He pointed out that Chrysler's health care cost per active employee was 400 percent higher than Japan's Mitsubishi Motors ($815 versus $5700) and that the gap was likely to increase. The Big Three auto companies spent $3.2 billion for health care that year. Today, we find that those depressing figures of 1984 have increased by about 12 percent.

This financial drain hurts us in many other areas of need. For instance, in 1950 government spending for health care was 45.9 percent of that of education; by 1984 it was equal to all government spending for education. Today, it is 10 percent greater.

We cannot honor these other commitments and continue to follow our current course of health care spending.

The already awesome numbers — in 1984 more than $1 billion a day was spent on health care — have continued to grow and consume a dramatically increasing portion of the gross national product. Health care in 1984 took 10.5 percent of the GNP. Now, in the 1990s, it consumes nearly 20 percent of our GNP. At the recent rate of increase, America could be spending 40 percent of the GNP on medical costs by 2013. This is absurd and devastating.

Morgenstern's first task was to persuade Americans that the current system couldn't continue. His second task was to show the inefficiency of the current system. America, he noted, spent more on health care than practically any other country in the world, and its system was so inefficient and wasteful that it didn't even deliver good health. "We are rated ninth among industrial countries in respect to general health and health care, yet we are second in spending. This expensive but inefficient system must be controlled."

His suggestions for reform were articulated in an address he delivered to Congress shortly after his State of the Union Message. The major theses of his health care message were:

1. That America had too many hospital beds. He furnished government statistics that showed there were between 100,000 and 200,000 hospital beds idle at any one time. "An empty hospital bed costs society but doesn't cure anyone," Morgenstern pointed out.

2. That many hospital facilities were used wastefully. "U.S. government estimates show that 30 percent of the people in hospital beds at any one time don't need to be there. They are there for the convenience of the patient's doctor or to satisfy a clause in the insurance policy," he argued. He pointed out that enrollees in health maintenance organizations had 40 percent fewer hospital admissions and days of hospitalization per capita than the fee-for-service population.

3. That America was training too many doctors. "The physician-to-population ratio in the United States increased from 140 per 100,000 to 200 per 100,000 and it is expected to increase substantially in the years ahead," said Morgenstern. He thereupon announced that he would use the power of his office to reduce all medical school admissions by 10 percent and stop the inflow of foreign medical school graduates.

4. That the United States used its technology inefficiently. Morgenstern proposed using the federal regulations on Medicare and Medicaid to insist that hospitals share expensive technology rather than duplicate existing machines in the same geographical area. "America cannot afford to equip every hospital with all the latest technology — all underutilized. We have only enough resources to pay for what patients need, not for what hospitals want."

5. That the medical profession was subject to too many lawsuits. "Doctors are not the ensurers of good results for their patients. Defensive medicine is too costly and

too inefficient, and doctors must be given more immunity from legal attack." Morgenstern proposed legislation that would eventually reduce the number of medical malpractice suits by one-half.

6. That the United States was spending too much on useless and often counterproductive procedures during the last few months of people's lives. "It makes no sense to spend so much of our medical resources forcing a few more painful days of life on hopelessly ill patients." Morgenstern proposed that each state adopt "living will" legislation allowing people the right to discontinue "heroic" methods of treatment if they were terminally ill and the machines would merely prolong dying.

7. That we needed a reformed health care system to meet new lifestyle and new health needs. "We cannot abuse our bodies, then bring them to the government to fix," said Morgenstern. "With due respect to the medical profession, the dramatic decline in the U.S. and international death rate is the result of public health victories over infectious diseases. The reforms in hygiene and the improvement in drinking water and sewage systems have done far, far more to improve national and international well-being than all the spending on health care. We would do much better to cut smoking in half than to double health spending."

The success of Morgenstern's campaign on this issue was proven in the reduction of health care expenditures to 8 percent of the GNP in 1995 (from a high of 20 percent in the early 1990s), combined with an overall increase in the health of the American public. Morgenstern himself, after he left office, considered the control of health care costs one of his major accomplishments. "We could not have revitalized our economy without controlling health care costs," he observed in his autobiography.

The health care issue illustrated Morgenstern's ability to look at the big picture. He saw clearly that health care was not an isolated issue unrelated to other crises of government, and that resources that were being wasted or inefficiently applied were badly needed in other sectors of the economy.

Morgenstern's handling of that issue also reflected his use of parables to get his point across. Leadership is the ability to communicate, to simplify, to illustrate. In stressing preventive medicine and the need for individuals to take more responsibility for their own health, he liked to tell this parable:

A Contemporary Parable: Upstream/Downstream

It has been many years since the first body was spotted in the river. Some old-timers in Downstream remember how spartan were the facilities and procedures for managing that sort of thing. Sometimes, they say, it would take hours to pull ten people from the river, and even then only a few would survive.

Though the number of victims in the river has increased greatly in recent years, the good folks of Downstream have responded admirably to the challenge. Their rescue system is clearly second to none: most people discovered in the swirling waters are reached within twenty seconds, many in less than ten. Only a small number drown each day before help arrives — a big improvement from the way it used to be.

Talk to the people of Downstream and they'll speak with pride about the new hospital by the edge of the water, the

flotilla of rescue boats ready for service at a moment's notice, the comprehensive health plans for coordinating all
the manpower involved, and the large number of highly
trained and dedicated swimmers always ready to risk their
lives to save victims from the raging currents. Sure it costs
a lot, but, say the Downstreamers, what else can decent
people do except provide whatever it takes when human
lives are at stake?

Oh, a few people in Downstream have raised the question
now and again, but most folks show little interest about
what's happening Upstream. It seems there's so much to do
to help those in the river that nobody's got time to check
how all those bodies are getting there in the first place.
That's the way things are, sometimes.*

Systems Thinking

One trait Martin Morgenstern had was his "integrative"
thinking, a trait with goals outside the trends of the American education system but that was indispensable to modern
leadership. During the 1970s and 1980s, universities, business, and government favored more specialization in a time
when generalists were, in fact, most important to solving
the complex problems the society faced. One contemporary of Morgenstern had observed, "If we are to retain any
command at all over the future, the ablest people we have
in every field must give thought to the largest problems of
the nation. They don't have to be in government to do so,
but they have to come out of the trenches of their own
speciality and look at the whole battlefield."

The American paradox of leadership was that one's du-
ties and responsibilities increased almost in direct proportion to one's ignorance. Or, as stated in the famous Peter

*From Donald B. Ardell, *High-level Wellness — An Alternative to Doctors, Drugs, and
Disease* (Emmaus, Pa.: Rodale Press, 1977).

Principle, someone with ability eventually will get promoted to a level too high — a "level of incompetence." A leader had to cut himself or herself off from the specialty of his or her training and observe the bigger picture. Morgenstern himself had a wide view of the United States and its problems, and he was unencumbered by a narrow specialty. An MIT-trained engineer, he had read widely in philosophy, classics, and history. It was not his formal education that enabled him to analyze the interplay of multiple factors, integrate them into a comprehensive whole, and make a decision.

Morgenstern did make a great contribution in his "systems analysis," especially in the areas of health care and defense. Shortly after his inauguration, Morgenstern set up two task forces to look at the systems that governed health and defense spending.

The fight on defense spending was the more costly to Morgenstern. Unlike health care, there was no groundwork laid on the systems problem inherent in defense spending. The dialogue was about individual weapons systems, rather than rational systems that produce intelligent and efficient defense strategies.

Morgenstern started his campaign for an "effective defense" by holding a press conference with five former chiefs of staff, led by Brigadier General David Jones, who attested to the inefficiencies in the current system. "The Joint Chiefs have no method for analyzing what a balanced defense system needs," Jones stated. "The very structure gets you the maximum wish list from every service. No one balances the whole; everyone gets their wish list."

Next came the "rank inflation" of the military. "In 1945," Jones stated, "the air force had 2.4 million men, 72,000 planes, and 298 generals. By 1958, the first two numbers had shrunk to 858,000 men and 27,000 aircraft, but we had 418 generals — that is, one general for every 64 planes. We now have one general for every 19 aircraft, not an efficient way to run either a railroad or an air force. Today, 50 percent *more* lieutenant colonels manage 25 percent *fewer* people and one-tenth the number of planes than at the end of World War II. The military must also pull in its belt. It is the industrial power and the technological strength of the United States and not the missile count that is the ultimate basis of our security."

"There is a crisis in governance," said Morgenstern. "We are spending too much money inefficiently and the answer is not the meat ax but the scalpel. We need to reduce spending not by blindly cutting budgets, but by revising our systems. We can learn to reach goals efficiently."

Unlike other Presidents, Morgenstern did not believe in the old ritual of appointing a blue-ribbon commission to study a problem, hailing its work when the final report came in, then quietly burying the results. The Medical Investigation Task Force he appointed — comprised of doctors with independent minds and a few administrative experts — went into the American hospital and health care system and emerged six months later with a report that became a blueprint for administration action.

As Morgenstern had advocated, it suddenly became very difficult for a foreign doctor to pass medical boards in the United States. Medical schools in universities, after having the chance to examine a whole new set of proposed federal rules about government grants and student loans, began to cut back enrollments. At the beginning of 1994, a nationwide computer system operated by the Department of Health and Human Services went into operation. It linked every hospital and clinic in the country to a medical clearinghouse in Chicago. There, a Cray III computer kept constant track of the whereabouts and availability of every specialist in the country. It also tracked the availability of every piece of special medical equipment. Finally, it recorded the status of every hospital bed in the country. It was the beginning of what was to become the National Resource-Efficiency System, which was to be one of Morgenstern's great legacies.

On the face of it, the battle to bring systems sanity to the Pentagon should have been the bloodiest of all, the Joint Chiefs being so strongly fortified and so many attempts having failed previously. Strangely, when the time came, the country seemed to welcome Morgenstern's initiative. The press discovered that, suddenly, all the years of enormous Reagan and Bush defense budgets seemed to have been building toward a great negative reaction from the public. The many scandals about favored contractors and huge cost overruns coincided with the now almost-proverbial examples such as that of the $7 hammer for which the air force had paid $600. When the new Congress began to examine the Department of Defense budget in 1993, congressmen began to hear from the voters back home as they had never heard before. Senators and representatives used to saluting whenever a general or admiral came to Capitol Hill for a budget hearing, suddenly turned into tigers. It took all of Morgenstern's skill to convey to Congress the idea that he did not wish to cut weapons systems and troop strengths wholesale. What he did want was a purchasing system run with a near-total dedication to honesty, frugality, and efficiency. Under Donald Stanton, the new secretary of defense, almost a thousand ranking army, navy, and air force officers chose retirement within two months. Several of the Pentagon whistle-blowers — demoted or fired by previous administrations — suddenly found themselves in high policy positions in logistics areas. Before long, computer programs were subjecting every expenditure and every use of human or technological resources to a cost-versus-product equation. As Stanton said in a press confer-ence, "It's just a lot harder to get approval to buy some-thing; it's a lot harder to get approval to junk anything or sell it off. But it's a lot easier to use what we have on hand."

It was several more years before systems analysis could be applied thoroughly and successfully to the Department of Defense, but Morgenstern's new administrative regula-tions, along with new legislation and enthusiastic support from the Congress, made some giant strides.

Morgenstern, as his first year in office passed, showed both the imagination of a leader and the common sense of a manager. He could inspire people toward goals and de-vise a practical plan for achieving them, as well as provide rational methods of cutting costs and at the same time not lose the mystique of leadership that supplied the energy to drive ahead.

Immigration

President Morgenstern waited until his economic and health care programs were in place before taking on the thorny subject of immigration. He had an acute sense of how much change even a politically sympathetic Congress could support at any one time. But once an economic re-building program was in place, he turned his attention to immigration.

In his 1994 State of the Union Message he called for an immigration reform package that would: (1) adopt em-ployer sanctions, at long last making it illegal to hire an illegal immigrant; (2) set a ceiling on legal immigration at 300,000 per year and include refugees within this ceiling; and (3) enact safeguards to ensure that illegal aliens do not have access to social services.

In that speech Morgenstern used a phrase that caught the attention of the media and summed up the public attitude. "What about our own huddled masses?" he asked the nation. "Don't we owe *them* the chance to breathe free?

"I would suggest that it is no longer in the interest of the country to have an uncontrolled growth in population," said Morgenstern. "It does not solve national problems; it makes their solution more difficult. It aggravates our resource scarcity, it overburdens our social services, it degrades our environment, and it helps ignite inflation."

On this issue, Morgenstern ran into some strong opposition both within and outside of Congress. It was argued that immigrants had built the country from its beginnings, that America had always opened its golden door to the oppressed and the dispossessed seeking freedom and opportunity. It was noted that many immigrants brought with them skills and talents that added to the national wealth.

Morgenstern replied that those arguments once made sense, but there is often a point when a tradition based on enlightened self-interest loses its validity. The world had changed. What was once an ideal was now becoming a dangerous sentimentality. He said that there was an even more fundamental American ideal: that of being able to create enough wealth to give everybody a share.

Finally, Morgenstern pointed out, in the years of great mass immigration, 1820 to 1930, the average number of new arrivals amounted to only 345,500 per year. Morgenstern would better that by more than half a million a year. And, he added, he would divide the quota between verifiable victims of disaster and repression and verifiably skilled and productive immigrants.

He never once mentioned the 12 percent unemployment rate, but that was probably the most telling argument in

Congress, where, toward the end of 1994, the Immigration Reform Act passed by a wide margin. It incorporated all that Morgenstern had asked for.

There were, of course, some hurt feelings among friendly nations when the much-reinforced Immigration and Naturalization Service swung into action in 1995. American citizens grumbled at the new passport requirements for trips to Mexico, Canada, and the Caribbean. And, although it was impossible to seal off all intrusion, the old porous borders were now much better protected. Illegal immigrants no longer sailed in, waded in, or got trucked in by the hundreds of thousands.

Morgenstern's election represented the triumph of a certain pragmatism that struck many Americans as cold and uncaring. "America has a duty to the world," thundered the Congressional Hispanic Caucus in the course of numerous demonstrations demanding dramatically increased immigration.

Morgenstern countered with the argument that Central America, the Caribbean, and South America combined were adding 4.5 million people to their labor force every year while the entire region had only one-third the GNP of the United States. "We must find ways to ensure the economic opportunity of our own citizens," argued Morgenstern at a press conference. "We cannot accept more people than our economy can accommodate and our society assimilate."

Foreign Aid

No policy of Morgenstern's was more controversial than his foreign aid and food policy. After he announced this in another landmark speech — this one to a meeting of the

National Council of Churches in October of his first year in
office — he was attacked from half the pulpits in the country. He was called cruel and heartless by opposing politicians and on numerous editorial pages. At his public ap-
pearances, the World Responsibility Movement demonstrated with hundreds of signs bearing the picture of
a starving African child and the legend "Morgenstern,
look!"

It was another sharp crisis of conscience for the American people. It brought the generous impulses that had
produced a century and a half of American missionary,
relief, and economic aid efforts into conflict with the tragic
reality that half the globe could not — and would not
— feed its peoples.

For his address, Morgenstern took as his theme the notion that God helps those who help themselves. Morgenstern began, "I do not come here to advocate cutting off
aid to countries in need. But I do come with a request to
limit that aid to countries that are in dire need and yet
will help themselves. Let me explain. You are the leader
of the Third World nation of Abcedia, say, and you
launch an all-out effort toward zero population growth,
including birth control education, and another all-out
effort to introduce agricultural reforms, increasing acreage
and new crops — in short, a heroic attempt to put resources and population in balance. If you are such a leader,
America will come to your aid, whether you are a socialist,
a dictator, or a hereditary monarch, because you are on the
side of history.

"If you reject these efforts to help yourself, do not expect
either God or the United States of America to interfere.
You are headed for the dustbin of history."

Other parts of this important policy speech are worth
quoting at length:

The geometry of population growth shatters our expectations for a better world. I was born in 1935. The population doubled, from 2.2 billion to 4.7 billion, in my first fifty years of life, and by the time I reach sixty-five there will be 6 billion people on earth. In 1984, the earth was gaining 150 new persons per minute; 9100 per hour; 218,100 per day; and 80 million per year! Seventy-three million of those are in the Third World. By 1995 we will be adding 90 million people a year to our finite globe and by 2020 mankind will total 7.8 billion people, 7 billion of them in the Third World.

Much of our population growth comes from the countries that can least support the additional people. They live in barrios, slums, villages, shantytowns, mud huts — and 800 million of them go to bed hungry.

We are losing the battle to raise people's living standards. Since the creation of the various OPEC cartels and mineral cartels, the world's economy has not grown as fast as the world's population. In many countries that means that living standards fall year after year and poverty slowly turns into abject poverty. Former ambassador Marshall Green, chairman of the National Security Council's Task Force on Population, showed the connection: "When you have a country like Bangladesh, where the population growth every year is over two million people, you have to have 400,000 more tons of grain, 700,000 more jobs, 300,000 more dwellings, and 11,000 more schools. How are you ever going to come up with the money necessary for development when these costs are so enormously high?"

This rapid population growth translates into the steady worsening of every major social problem: unemployment, massive urbanization, pressure on food supplies, degradation of the environment, increase in poverty.

One in ten children in poor countries dies before its first birthday. Fourteen point eight million children under five die every year — mostly from hunger and malnutrition.

Seven hundred fifteen million children in the less-developed countries aren't in school. Eight hundred million people are illiterate. One billion people lack clean drinking water; two billion lack sanitary facilities; one-fourth of the world lives in makeshift shelters.

Since 1960, the world has seen its working-age population (fifteen to sixty-four years of age) increase by 1.88 billion. Between 1960 and 1980 it increased by 730 million, and between 1980 and 2000 it will have increased by 1.15 billion. In the succeeding twenty years, we will add almost another billion and a half people, most of whom will be condemned to marginal existence jobs, if they can find employment at all.

By the year 2000, two billion people, or one-third of the world's total population, will live in countries with a gross national product averaging less than $250 per person per year. Those people who live in that abject poverty outnumber the people in the United States, Western Europe, Canada, and Australia combined.

Though the worldwide birthrate has dropped slightly, in Bangladesh, Pakistan, Africa, and a number of Moslem countries — about 20 percent of the world — we have seen no drop in the birthrate. In the other 80 percent there has been a slight drop. That is hardly "good news."

Even if economic growth rates were 6 percent a year (wildly optimistic) and even if birthrates dropped rapidly (a Pollyanna-ish prediction), that would still leave hundreds of millions of people in abject poverty and starvation.

The conditions of revolution are widespread and growing. There is a desperate mismatch between the rising expectations and the resources to meet those expectations. High birthrates, urbanization, corruption as a way of life, and the vast discrepancy between rich and poor are laying the groundwork for political earthquakes of gargantuan proportions. Developing countries are seeing young people pushed off the land by environmental degradation, unequal ownership, or economic stagnation. Those young people come to cities that can hardly provide for the numbers already there. As the September 1983 report of the Population Crisis Committee said of these international powder kegs:

> The developing world's rapid evolution into an urban society concentrates much of its disproportionately large youth population in congested slum areas close to the seats of power. The cities in turn provide the intellectual leadership and the social stimulus for mass mobilization of unemployed, disaffected youth. Urbanization also increases access to modern communication, which magnifies the inequities within and between countries and publicizes political movements in other countries. Leaders of developing countries view with alarm the increased potential for organized violence emerging from this combustible combination of demographic and social factors, threatening the process of orderly political change even in countries with a commitment to social reform. The leaders of the Western powers, against whom political rhetoric and violence are often directed, may also have cause for concern.*

Most developing countries are filled with hungry people, 60 percent of whom are malnourished and many of whom are starving. Unemployment and underemployment are incalculable, but clearly above 50 percent, and those who work receive subsistence wages. Health care is minimal. Illiteracy rates, many times, are between 60 and 80 percent. Large urban areas, filled with festering slums without adequate sanitation or electricity or water, are the ruined remains of once beautiful cities.

Even if the United States were to try to feed the world, we couldn't do so for long. We would soon find that even if there were food enough for this type of massive export, it would not be possible to transport enough of it. Additional food production could never keep up with a world

*The report is entitled "World Population Growth and Global Security."

population that increases by 90 million each year. All these mouths are added to a world already requiring 40 million metric tons of grain annually.

Studies show, moreover, that American food aid has enabled recipient governments to put off the hard decisions about how to feed their own population, allowing their food deficits to grow, year after year. The United States, in effect, made the situation worse by dumping food into the markets of hungry nations. The result was a depression in prices and elimination of profits for farmers in those countries, which actually increased the number of hungry people.

Major Accomplishments

The eight years of the Morgenstern administration had their fierce battles, their failures, and their successes. Martin Morgenstern, like Franklin Roosevelt, the President he most resembled, had warned that there was no easy road to national recovery. Probably his most striking accomplishment was to convince most of the American people that was true. Partly through force of personality and partly through the unavoidable evidence of things around him, he was able to convey the image of a country very much like the *Titanic* — a rich and wasteful luxury liner — steaming heedlessly toward a collision. Then, in a triumph of persuasion, he succeeded in convincing the nation that the collision was not inevitable. The liner could reduce its speed, use better lookout tactics, take evasive action when necessary.

These were the major accomplishments of the Morgenstern administration:

The U.S. economy regained a basic kind of health under the Morgenstern revitalization program. The national plant began to undergo drastic modernization — with computerized and robotized industry replacing many of the obsolescent smokestack factories. With tax-break encouragement and a shrewd system of subsidy (along with a deliberate weakening of the dollar in international exchange), American business began to regain foreign markets — and, as a result, the balance of payments deficit was reduced dramatically in the years 1993 through 2000.

The great overhaul of the social-governmental system began to show remarkable results. The whole health care and medical system underwent a much-needed shrinkage — and, as Morgenstern had predicted, without any deleterious effects on the general health of the populace.

The reform of not just the Social Security system but the whole American retirement system was revolutionary, but by the end of the century, the benefits were becoming obvious. All military pensions were transferred to Social Security, an action that not only saved large sums but helped to inhibit double dipping. A means test and a moderate tax on retirement income beyond the maximum Social Security benefit figure helped to keep the system in the black.

The whole complex of American education received a new impetus. Nothing of the sort had happened in the field since the post-Sputnik energizing under President John F. Kennedy. Congress voted generous new funds for pure science, for all the applied sciences, for engineering, and for research and development. It quickly became more rewarding for students to choose graduate work in science or math over law or medicine. The humanities — having had little subsidy before — remained largely unaffected.

In a speech to the Vocational Teachers Association, Morgenstern stated: "There is nothing more dangerous to a twenty-first-century nation than ignorance. Education for the individual is emancipation; for the country it is the key to progress and economic success. The trouble with mankind is not that they ate of the tree of knowledge, but that they did not eat enough. The renaissance of our nation will be led by education."

The new President's immigration and naturalization policies, after much heated debate, gained acceptance.

Crimes of violence and street crime had been declining during the late 1980s and continued to decline after Morgenstern took office. His main attack was directed against organized crime, particularly the tendency of organized crime to absorb legitimate businesses. In this regard, the Justice Department's vigorous drive against the laundering of illegally gained money produced striking results in the mid-1990s.

The Environmental Protection Agency, which had lost much of its effectiveness under Presidents Reagan and Bush, got new funds and new enforcement authority under Morgenstern. The favoritism toward private enterprise at the expense of the public interest was reversed.

High on Morgenstern's priority list had been a gigantic project to renew the infrastructure of the United States — including obsolescent roads and highways, bridges, rail lines, and port facilities. This he undertook late in his first term when the improved deficit picture began to permit the initial expenditures. This project remains ongoing.

None of this would have been possible, however, without the tremendous national sacrifice to balance budgets and reduce the national debt. Part of this triumph can be attributed to the charismatic way in which Morgenstern made fiscal questions urgent and dramatic. Other candidates in the past had warned and deplored without much effect. But, as the *Washington Post* put it, "Morgenstern, in his inaugural address, commanded enough eloquence to make just about every listener feel as if he had suddenly gone broke. The President, for the first time since the advent of John Maynard Keynes, made every person feel that his country's debt was his own. But the truly remarkable effect, as every subsequent opinion poll has shown, was to mobilize the national will behind Morgenstern's 'reality therapy' — the new austerity program he offers.''

It was not the new President alone. Events of the previous twelve years had had a cumulative effect that no one could overlook. The first four years of the Reagan administration had piled up federal deficits of more than half a trillion dollars. Despite new taxes in the second term, the second Reagan administration and the Bush administration added more than another half trillion. But, suddenly, there was a new determination to do something about this. One had to look back to the beginning of Roosevelt's New Deal or to World War II to find an equivalent for the kind of unity the country showed in its support for President Morgenstern.

Along with that, he had the help of perhaps the most brilliant governmental and legislative team in recent history. Morgenstern chose most of his Cabinet (except such officers as the secretary of state and the attorney general) on the basis of their knowledge of economics and shrewdness in fiscal management. Many White House advisers had the same qualifications — in fact, the press soon revived the Roosevelt-era nickname Brain Trust for Morgenstern's mixed team of professorial and managerial types.

He was equally fortunate in his congressional leadership. The landslide of 1992 carried to Washington an actual majority in both houses of young, progressive, able legislators. Congress members in almost unprecedented numbers crossed party lines to support the administration's proposals.

It was an enormous boost to morale when Morgenstern

was able not only to balance the budget but to carry a $4 billion surplus during his second term in office. Although economists continue to estimate that reduction of the national debt to an acceptable figure will not be accomplished for another ten years, Morgenstern had renamed the *Titanic,* had slowed her speed, had set her on a new and favorable course, and had installed radar to detect icebergs.

PART THREE

The Time of Peace

The following pages are an excerpt from *A Contemporary History,* by Richard Sharp. Boston: Houghton Mifflin Company, 2020.

The time of peace ultimately came not through the brotherhood of man but through the terror of example. Peace was a product not of religion or arms control. Instead it came through a brutal realization of the vulnerability of society and the fragility of man.

History shows periods of peace to be the exception rather than the rule. Since the dawn of history, nation has fought nation, tribe has fought tribe, village has fought village, neighbor has fought neighbor. The history of man is partially written in blood — construction giving way to destruction, peace and stability turning into war and chaos. Wars were as inevitable to history as storms were to weather.

As the twentieth century, already history's most destructive period, lurched to a close, violence and terrorism increased dramatically. Faction against faction, religion against religion, country against country, the violence seemed to reach a crescendo. The Soviet Union and the United States both instituted "launch on warning" nuclear systems. A myriad of regional wars, religious and sectarian strife, terrorism, and random acts of violence were daily communicated to a weary and cynical world. Peace was a stranger. Man seemed to have lost his capacity to be shocked.

One American wit seemed to sum up the dilemma: "More than any other time in history, mankind faces the crossroads. One path leads to despair and utter hopelessness, the other to total extinction. I pray we have the wisdom to choose wisely."

The flash point came, with history's usual irony, in the least expected place. Though India and Pakistan had fought three wars (1947, 1965, and 1971), an uneasy truce had existed between them. Theirs was a legacy of hate and distrust, but no significant increase in tensions is known to have preceded the devastating nuclear exchange. None of history's usual causations seemed to apply to the conflagration: no jihad, no territorial dispute, no recent reason for revenge. History's most bloody war was apparently caused by a minor miscalculation. As with the War of Jenkins' Ear, the cause appeared almost insignificant. Lost in the radiated ashes, it conjured up Hannah Arendt's phrase "the banality of evil." No communication from either country harbingered the holocaust. It just happened.

The morning of November 29, 2005, dawned clear and cool over the Indian subcontinent. The harvests had been sparse, but adequate. The border between India and Pakistan, long the scene of minor incidents, had been exceptionally quiet.

True, the religious differences were as strong as ever, but no known incident or aggravation was present. November 29 was like so many similar days — alive with pungent smells, buzzing women on the way to market, mischievous children at play, men toiling in the fields. True, the Hindus worshiped many gods while the Moslems worshiped one. True also, the Moslems eschewed pork and were quiet in church while the Hindus proscribed beef and had music in their church. More to the point, both shared a legacy of religious strife and conflict that defied even a peacemaker such as Gandhi and resulted in the partition of the subcontinent. But nothing in the mind or imagination of man could have justified or explained a spasm of hate equal to what came to be called the Great Annihilation.

Simply put, one moment hundreds of millions of people were going about their daily routines and the next moment they were ashes. For historical accuracy, it must be pointed out that satellite photographs confirm that India was attacked first, but the immediacy of the response gives rise to the speculation that both nations may have been on alert for some time. It is impossible to assign "blame," and even the concept seems irrelevant to the horror that followed.

What is important to note is the unpredictability of events and how easily one minor event can lead to another, with increasing speed and significance, until a human chain reaction causes a nuclear chain reaction. Just as an assassination in Sarajevo started a chain of events, one following inevitably after another, it is likely that on the Indian subcontinent some small slight led to an insult, an insult to an incident, an incident to an outrage, and an outrage to the holocaust. Events soon passed beyond all human control. The "guns of August" became the "missiles of November."

"If the iron dice must roll, may God help us," declared an anguished Theobald von Bethmann-Hollweg on August 1, 1914. Eighty years later, the nuclear dice rolled, on a scale that eclipsed even the destruction of two world wars. But it did something more important. It made absurd such concepts as "winners" and "losers" in modern warfare. President Elizabeth Dole, in her characteristic way, put it succinctly: "Winning a nuclear war is like saying, 'Your end of the boat is sinking!' "

The total devastation wrought by nuclear weapons was made clear by the absence of reports emanating from either Pakistan or India. The first indications came from American and Russian satellites, which reported that a nuclear exchange had taken place and that at least twenty nuclear weapons had been detonated. But death ruled the subcontinent. No "stop the presses" telegram like the one from Sarajevo; no similarity to the cacophony of reports from Pearl Harbor: the first sound of this war was silence. Chilling, eerie silence.

Then a few confused messages were transmitted. Something significant had taken place. "Multiple blinding flashes seen to the northwest," radioed Colombo, Sri Lanka. From Mangalore, India, a radio operator sent word of "large mushroom clouds from Bangalore and Madras."

If there was a moment one could pinpoint that the Time of Peace began, it would be when the first TV reports burst upon a world that had thought itself beyond shock. The first pictures were taken from the air by network news crews aboard leased airplanes hurriedly flown to India from Sri Lanka and Thailand. The first vague images were of a moonlike landscape, with nothing standing but charred rubble. Press reports repeated the words from the *Bhagavad-Gita* that J. Robert Oppenheimer spoke after observing the first successful atomic test: "I am become death, the destroyer of worlds." Here was a world destroyed.

From television sets all over the globe came the mind-boggling footage. Craters where last week cities stood. Cinders who a few days before had laughed and loved. Children with seared flesh who had been twenty miles from an inferno called an epicenter. A myriad of people struck blind, whose only mistake had been to look at the fireball. In every country, city, town, village, barrio, ghetto, and favela, the universality of suffering was dramatically played out before the shocked eyes of all who could bear to look.

Peace thus came not through treaty but through example. The goal of peace was no longer the purview of politicians alone — it became a demand of every citizen. If war was too important to be left to generals, peace became a groundswell that swept over politicians of all nationalities. The demonic horror of the Indian subcontinent brought home to all the universality not of brotherhood but of the vulnerability of man. Man got a chance to look into the abyss and he was horrified beyond words. No religious or national goals could justify destruction and desolation on this scale. War was mutual suicide. The message went not only to the head but to the heart. As Aeschylus said so well:

> Even in our sleep
> Pain that we cannot forget
> Falls drop by drop upon the heart
> Until in our own despair
> Against our will
> Comes wisdom
> Through the awful grace of God.

One is cynically tempted to cite Tacitus: "Where they make a desert, they call it peace." The aphorism would seem appropriate if restricted to the survivors of India and Pakistan. Those two countries, left with a desert, were too exhausted and traumatized to fight. They could only suffer. Hundreds of millions of refugees in both countries rushed to escape the fallout. Survival was determined by the caprice of the winds.

But this "desert" aphorism misses the symbolic value of the horror. It ignores the vividness of the pictures sent around the world. Unlike Carthage, whose destruction was witnessed by few, the Great Annihilation was witnessed by all. The grim pictures of the widespread suffering were transmitted to the far corners of the globe. The whole world saw the desert — the suffering of the people caught in radiated rain as their hair fell out, as bruises appeared on their bodies, as they began to bleed from ears, noses, and mouths. But worst of all was watching the children die. Helpless, guilty of no sins save those of their fathers, they died horrible radiation deaths. The survivors envied the dead. In a thousand languages and dialects, people of different faiths recognized, "There, but for the grace of God, go I."

As if to drive the point home came the Years Without Summer. The nuclear explosions and resulting fires put large quantities of fine dust and soot into the atmosphere and changed the climate of the entire Northern Hemisphere. Tests showed that, in addition, the ozone layer of the atmosphere, which shields man from the malignant ultraviolet radiation, had been permanently damaged. Nuclear war was Hydra-headed: first the catastrophe of the blast; then the devastation of the fallout; then the climatic disaster of a nuclear winter; and, finally, after the soot and dust had settled out, the continuing curse of ultraviolet radiation.

No formal arms control agreement followed the holocaust. Politicians continued to find barriers to treaties. There were always technical problems and difficulties of ensuring compliance. But peace is neither the absence of war nor the presence of a disarmament agreement. Peace is a change of heart.

There were, as always, other factors that supplemented the change of heart. Both the United States and the Soviet Union were increasingly frustrated by the resources going into the arms race. Each had to match the other, but the cost was high. Both had built a nuclear Maginot Line: an awesomely expensive but unusable defense system. This system gave little military security and that even at the expense of economic security. Both nations were suffering domestically because of the resources put into the military.

They were losing the economic race while struggling to win the arms race.

The United States was allocating 40 percent of its scientists and 7 percent of its GNP to the military. Its previous role as world economic leader was suffering severely. Once the leader in per capita income, by 1994 it was down to seventh place. Once the world's leading exporter, it had become the world's leading importer with a devastating negative balance of trade. Once the financier of the world, since 1987 it had been a debtor nation. America was an economic giant crippled by the costs of defense and an economy that had lost its magic.

The Soviet Union was similarly beset. Their expensive nuclear arsenal was no help for their real problems, which included a billion Chinese on one border who hated them; an unwon and unwinnable war in Afghanistan; a military machine that took 15 percent of their GNP; massive dissatisfaction among their satellites; a history of bad harvests; the highest alcoholism rate in the world; and increasing ethnic strife in the south.

Like two clumsy, muscle-bound fighters eyeing each other suspiciously, the two superpowers added useless missile upon useless missile while other sectors of their economy suffered and while living standards started to decline. The peace process, once started, also became an economic issue. The Time of Peace arrived because the costs of war in economic and human terms became manifest.

One additional result completes the picture: the Adopt a Refugee program. So many children were orphaned, so many needed extraordinary medical care, that the developed world agreed to take in these children for treatment and adoption. The one international effort that did succeed was the Save the Children conference organized by Switzerland. There the Russians made the dramatic announcement that the Soviet Union would match the United States in accepting these children. All nations took in some of the injured, and these children were spread throughout the world, serving as a grim reminder of the human costs of breaking the peace.

Peace came not from the efforts of the actors on the world stage who had failed so often, but through a preview of coming events. It was not idealism or love of mankind that brought peace, but the reality of war. It was not the morality or immorality of war, but the price of war. It was not the abstract odds of war, but the recognition of the devastating stakes. Man looked into the abyss and saw an irradiated Hell and recoiled in horror. Both the head and the heart came to realize that war was mutual suicide that would destroy not only nations but the species. The cost was high, but in the end, reality was the only effective teacher.

Epilogue

I believe there is a fundamental question in this book as to whether a democracy addicted to excesses can reform itself. To my mind, the question is a long way from being resolved.

In his book *Democracy in Decline?* political scientist Ralph Buultjens suggests:

> As capitalism matures and the consumer economy develops, the goods it produces tend to promote a wasteful and hedonistic society. This, in turn, leads to a weakening of the values necessary to maintain an energetic capitalist environment and promotes listless, unrestrained or apathetic attitudes. The rugged entrepreneurial spirit dissipates into dependency on government, and the vigor and intellectual imagination that sustains progress is lost . . . There is little doubt that the long-term future of capitalistic society and its allied political ethos is largely dependent on its capacity to recover its sense of purpose.

I sincerely believe that America has built up expectations beyond our ability to deliver and that our economy is heading toward an immense dislocation. America pretends it can solve its problems without sacrifice, without hard choices.

Alas, there are no solutions without some hard choices and sacrifice. In some areas, such as health care, we could spend our dollars so much more efficiently that we could offer more people better care for less money. There the dilemma is getting the reform started. But in other areas, such as the federal deficit, immigration, entitlement reform, and election reform, there will be no alternative without pain. All alternatives involve some need for shared sacrifice. In so many areas American institutions have grown flaccid, bureaucratic, incestuous, lazy. America needs a revitalization based not on false optimism but on realism.

In his book *The Public Philosophy*, Walter Lippmann described the political dynamic in a democracy of raising unpleasant facts.

> At the critical moments in this sad history, there have been men, worth listening to, who warned the people against their mistakes. Always, too, there have been men inside the governments who judged correctly, because they were permitted to know in time, the uncensored and unvarnished truth. But the climate of modern democracy does not usually inspire them to speak out. For what Churchill did in the Thirties before Munich was exceptional: the general rule is that a democratic politician had better not be right too soon. Very often the penalty is political death. It is much safer to keep in step with the parade of opinion than to try to keep up with the swifter movement of events.

The United States is full of politicians who hide the truth from the public and often from themselves. We break the rules of history, economics, and the social sciences and hope that, for the first time in history, we shall not have to pay the price. This is insanity. This is the politics of decline.

America is still a great nation. The traumas outlined in

this book can be avoided or minimized. We can face the future realistically and still have a high standard of living. If we move fast enough we can solve our national challenges.

It is my prayer that someone is listening.

Sources
Index

Sources

Part I: The Facts of Life in A.D. 2000

The Economy

Speech by the Secretary of the Treasury to the U.S. Chamber of Commerce
The subject of the American economy is much commented upon from various viewpoints. I was impressed by Lester C. Thurow's *The Zero-Sum Society* (Basic Books, New York, 1980), as well as by *The Real World War* by Hunter Lewis and Donald Allison (Coward, McCann and Geoghegan, New York, 1982) and Robert B. Reich's *The Next American Frontier* (New York Times Books, New York, 1983). *Global Stakes: The Future of High Technology in America,* by James Botkin, Dan Dimancescu, and Ray Stata (Ballinger Publishing Company, Cambridge, Mass., 1982), is also useful. *The Illusion of Conventional Economics,* by William H. Miernyk (West Virginia University Press, Morgantown, W. Va., 1982), is a critique of our current economic policies. *Time* magazine's "That Monster Deficit" (March 5, 1984) supplied some of the facts. Martin Feldstein's essay "How to Get the Deficit Under a Hundred Billion" in *Time*'s February 4, 1985, issue is the source of an instructive viewpoint and some helpful statistics. I believe

Martin Feldstein to have been the one intellectually honest official in the Reagan administration. I also enjoyed *Dangerous Currents: The State of Economics,* by Lester C. Thurow (Random House, New York, 1983), and Bob Kuttner's *The Economic Illusion* (Houghton Mifflin, Boston, 1984). The single most politically effective material on the budget is available from the Bipartisan Budget Appeal, Box 9, New York, New York 10004. This organization is chaired with great judgment and skill by Peter G. Peterson, former secretary of commerce. He is currently chairman of the board of Lehman Brothers Kuhn Loeb and one of the organizers of the Bipartisan Budget Appeal, along with five former secretaries of the treasury.

The National Governors' Association (Hall of the States, 444 North Capitol Street, Washington, D.C. 20001) has twice taken a strong and politically risky stand on the budget deficit and the economy. Its various publications on the federal budget were also helpful and timely.

I found the productivity figures in "Restoring Productivity Growth in America: A Challenge for the 1980s," a Report to the President of the United States and the Secretary of the Treasury by the National Productivity Advisory Committee (Washington, D.C., December 1983).

A useful piece on entitlements is Peter G. Peterson's "No More Lunch for the Middle Class" (*New York Times Magazine,* January 17, 1982).

"The Twilight of Smokestack America" by Peter T. Kilborn (*New York Times,* May 8, 1983) and "Can Smokestack America Rise Again?" by Gene Bylinsky (*Fortune,* February 6, 1984) provided me with some valuable information.

Dated but still pertinent is "The Shrinking Standard of Living" (*Business Week,* January 28, 1980).

The average monthly salary in 2000 and the price of an average single-family home are simple extrapolations of wages and prices if inflation continues at approximately the rate that it did during the 1970s. "The Incredible Shrinking Dollar," an article in a financial report, *The Money Advocate,* Vol. IV, no. 3, February 1984 (available at 4180 W. Broadway, Minneapolis, Minn. 55442) contains some good inflation projections, and I also used in my text their three options that face politicians. The federal deficit projections are simple extrapolations of present trends. Harry Truman added $4.4 billion to the federal deficit; Dwight Eisenhower added $15.8 billion; Kennedy and Johnson accumulated $53.9 billion; Nixon and Ford added $19.3 billion; Jimmy Carter added $101 billion; and Reagan added $735 billion in his first term alone.

Memorandum to the President from the Secretary of Commerce
Robert B. Reich's *The Next American Frontier* (New York Times Books, New York, 1983) addresses the trade problem facing the United States. The economic Darwinism that may or may not be at work in our society is well articulated in *The Work Revolution*, by Dr. Gail Schwartz (Rawson Associates, New York, 1983), and in "Storm Clouds on the Horizon, Labor Market Crisis and Industrial Policy," a publication of the Economic Education Project (152 Aspinwall Avenue, Suite 2, Brookline, Mass. 02146), by Barry Bluestone, Bennett Harrison, and Lucy Gorham. A study on how few high-tech jobs and how many service jobs there will be in the future has been published by Russell Rumberger and Harry M. Levin of the Stanford Institute for Research on Educational Finance in Government (Stanford University News Service, Stanford, Calif. 94305; April 27, 1984). Michael Harrington's "U.S. Next Economic Crisis" (*New York Times,* January 15, 1984) contained some noteworthy information on how new jobs "skidded" down the occupational ladder. One study that provided background for the material on the world economy and the international job gap is "Immigration and the Job Gap," published in November 1983 by the Environmental Fund (1320 18th Street N.W., Washington, D.C. 20036). Related to this subject is a symposium titled "Do We Need an Industrial Policy?" in the February 1985 issue of *Harper's*.

See also:

William E. Brock. "Trade and Debt: the Vital Linkage" (*Foreign Affairs,* Summer 1984).

Arthur F. Burns. "The American Trade Deficit in Perspective" (Department of State Bulletin, July 1984, pp. 55–59).

Robert Heilbroner. "Reflections (the Deficit)" (*The New Yorker,* July 30, 1984, pp. 47–55).

Memorandum to the President from the Chief U.S. Trade Negotiator
The best reference materials on Japanese trade barriers and the imbalance in U.S.-Japan trade are:

"America's High-Tech Crisis" (*Business Week,* March 11, 1985, pp. 56–67).

"Global Competition: The New Reality," a report of the President's Commission on Industrial Competitiveness (Volume I, January 1985).

"Japanese Barriers to U.S. Trade and Recent Japanese Government Trade Initiatives," Office of the U.S. Special Trade Representative, November 1982. (Submitted to the House of Representatives Committee on Foreign Affairs.)

Lohr, Steve. "The Japanese Challenge" (*New York Times Magazine,* July 8, 1984).

"Progress Report: 1984," a September 1984 report of the U.S.-Japan Study Group, a bilateral group consisting mainly of Americans from the U.S. business community in Tokyo and Japanese businessmen. A balanced and low-key summary of Japanese trade barriers.

Ulmer, Lionel. "Perspectives on U.S.-Japan Trade" (*Business America,* November 12, 1984).

See also:

Davidson, William H. *The Amazing Race* (John Wiley & Sons, New York, 1984). A good discussion of trade.

Fukushima, Glen S. "The Hidden Gap in U.S.-Japan Relations" (*Christian Science Monitor,* January 2, 1985).

Health Care

Speech by the Secretary of Health and Human Services to the Association for a Better New York
A very important book on health care is Alain C. Enthoven's *Health Plan* (Addison-Wesley, Reading, Mass., 1980). A good view of the international perspective on the health care crisis is *A Healthy State,* by Victor and Ruth Sidel (Pantheon, New York, 1983). The specter of rationing health care is raised in *The Painful Prescription: Rationing Hospital Care,* by Henry J. Aaron and William B. Schwartz (A Brookings Study in Social Economics, The Brookings Institution, Washington, D.C., 1984). See also *Medical Nemesis,* by Ivan Illich (Pantheon, New York, 1976), and *The Physician's Covenant, Images of the Healer in Medical Ethics,* by William F. May (The Westminster Press, Philadelphia, 1983). *The Economist* has had several articles on health care, in particular "Health Care International, Better Care at One-eighth the Cost?" (April 28, 1984) and "Time for à Tourniquet on Medical Costs" (February 2, 1985). Another good article is "Two Tiers of Care: The Unthinkable Meets the Inevitable" by Emily Friedman (*Trustee Magazine,* Vol. 37, no. 11, November 1984).

In general, the *New England Journal of Medicine* is a good source on this topic. See, for example, "Sounding Board: Learning to Say No" by Lester Carl Thurow (Vol. 311, no. 24, December 1984). Various speeches by Joseph Califano contain a great deal of insight into the problem of health care cost containment. One in particular that I used is "The Great Health Care Shell Game" (reprinted in the *National Association for Uniformed Services,* Vol. 8, no. 6, November-December 1984).

See also Clement Bezold's "Health Care in the U.S.: Four Alternative Futures" and Trevor Hancock's "Beyond Health Care" (both in *The Futurist,* August 1982).

Memorandum to the President from the Surgeon General
A series of community-level conferences seeking a balance between health costs and services in Oregon was sponsored by a
nonprofit organization called Bioethics Conference, Inc. (Department of Public Health and Preventive Medicine, Oregon
Health Sciences University). These conferences culminated in
January 1985 in a final report, "Society Must Decide." In addition, each interim report is a publication about ethics in health
care choices, which apply to all states.

"A Prisoner in the ICU: The Tragedy of William Bartling," by
George J. Annas, J.D., M.P.H. (*The Hastings Center Report,* December 1984), gives an important viewpoint. The difference between
statistical lives and identifiable lives is put forth in an op-ed piece
in the *New York Times* (April 25, 1980) called "Statistical Lives,"
which argues that we actually turn our backs on those we can't
televise. "The Irresistible Medical Technologies: Weighing the
Costs and Benefits," by Harvey Fineberg, in the November-
December 1984 *Technology Review,* also addresses that subject.
The commentary "Death Is Not the Enemy" in the *Journal of the
American Medical Association* (November 2, 1984, Vol. 252, no. 17)
makes similar important points. "Future Shock: The Six-Million-
Dollar Man May Have Gotten Off Cheap," by Spencer Rich, in
the *Washington Post National Weekly* (July 9, 1984), gives statistics
on projections for artificial organs. "Life, Death and the Dollar
Sign" in the *Journal of the American Medical Association* (July 13,
1984, Vol. 252, no. 2) also expands upon that theme.

Leon Kass's "The Case for Mortality" in *The American Scholar,*
Vol. 52, no. 2 (Spring 1983), contains a persuasive argument for
rethinking our health care priorities.

At the other end of the life spectrum, see Robert and Peggy
Stinson, *The Long Time Dying of Baby Andrew* (Atlantic–Little,
Brown, Boston, 1984).

The figures used here are 1984 figures and were not ex-
trapolated to the year 2000.

Tenets of the Eskimo Society
The Hemlock Society, P.O. Box 66218, Los Angeles, Calif. 90066, has a series of publications on the right to suicide and related issues, including "Let Me Die Before I Wake" by Derek Humphrey. *On Death with Dignity,* by Patrick F. Sheely, M.D. (Pinnacle Books, New York, 1981), *Concerning Death: A Practical Guide for the Living,* edited by Earl A. Grollman (Beacon Press, Boston, 1974), and *Counseling the Dying,* by Margaretta K. Bowers (Harper & Row, San Francisco, 1981), are all enlightening books on this topic.

Of the many books treating the subject of death with dignity, a handful were extremely important in the development of my thinking. Among them are *Morals in Medicine,* by Joseph Fletcher (Beacon Press, Boston, 1954), and *Good Life, Good Death: A Doctor's Case for Euthanasia and Suicide,* by Christiaan Barnard, M.D. (Prentice-Hall, Englewood Cliffs, N.J., 1980). The classic in the field of death and dying remains Elisabeth Kübler-Ross's *On Death and Dying* (Macmillan, New York, 1976). It is still very relevant, as is *The Way We Die: Investigation on Death and Dying in America Today,* by David Dempsey (McGraw-Hill, New York, 1977).

"The Right to Live, the Right to Die," in the *Stanford Magazine* (Spring 1983), is but one of the many articles on this subject. Fifth in a series of occasional papers published by the Population Reference Bureau is "Death and Taxes: The Public Policy Impact of Living Longer," edited by Paola M. Scommengna (September 1984); it is a very challenging, yet disturbing study on the economic impact of living longer and the cost-benefit ratios involved in curing various diseases.

Pensions

Memorandum to the President from the Re-election Committee
A series of articles on the elderly in America appears in the *Wilson Quarterly*, in the New Year's 1985 issue. Other articles include "A Granny Crisis Is Coming" (*The Economist*, May 19, 1984) and "The Elderly as a Class No Longer Poor" (*Denver Post*, January 19, 1983). "Looking Forward to Retiring and Living a Life of Ease? Don't," by Jarold A. Kieffer (*Washington Post National Weekly*, September 24, 1984), is excellent, as is "Pandering to the Elderly," by Terry Hartle (*Washington Post National Weekly*, August 13, 1984). An article by Ronald Kotulak and Lea Donosky, "Americans Pay Dearly for Their Longer Lives," appeared in the *Chicago Tribune* (September 9, 1984), and "Ever More Americans Live into the Eighties and Nineties, Causing Big Problems" appeared in the *Wall Street Journal* (July 30, 1984). An article comparing the rise in the number of elderly and the increasing burden on children is "Children and Elderly in the U.S.," by Samuel Preston, in *Scientific American* (December 1984). *The Futurist* issue of June 1984 featured a number of articles about the elderly; the topic of "Force Number One of the Ten Forces Shaping America" (*U.S. News & World Report*, March 19, 1984) is a maturing society. *Barron's* for May 28, 1984, contains an article by Gary Weiss, "Excellent Prognosis: The Outlook for Nursing Home Changes Glowing," which sets forth the demographics and economics of aging. See also "Life Spans of 200 Years Will Shatter Society" (*Denver Post*, June 17, 1982), by Marvin Cetron and Thomas O'Toole.

Memorandum to the President from the Director of the Office of Management and Budget

For some informational material on pensions, see John Bickerman's "The Military Payoff" (Center on Budget and Policy Priorities, February 1985).

The best material that I've seen on military retirements is from the Center on Budget and Policy Priorities, 236 Massachusetts Ave. N.E., Suite 305, Washington, D.C. 20002.

The July 18, 1983, *Christian Science Monitor* has a relevant article, "Military Pensions: A Political Minefield for Reformers," by Brad Knickerbocker, as does the July 9, 1984, *U.S. News & World Report*, "Behind the New Furor over Military Pensions." "Veterans Administration Goal: Model Care for Nine Million Older Veterans" appears in the June 4, 1984, *U.S. News & World Report*. See also "Veterans' Health Care Bill to Grow (*Wall Street Journal*, August 28, 1984); "The Old Soldier Problem That Won't Fade Away," by Pete Earley (*Washington Post National Weekly*, August 6, 1984); and "Budget Battle Shapes Up over Benefits for Veterans" (*New York Times*, February 3, 1985). "The Golden Ratchet," by Tony Sargent (*Enterprise Magazine*, September 1983), sets forth the cumulative cost of federal pensions, as does a speech by George Marotta, "The Growing Power of Senior Citizens" (reprinted in the May 1, 1983, issue of *Vital Speeches of the Day*, Vol. XLIX, no. 14).

Appointed by the President to do an exhaustive examination of federal spending, the Grace Commission released a report called *The President's Private Sector Survey on Cost Control* (Government Document No. Pr 40.8: C82, Government Printing Office, Washington, D.C., 1984). The commission found that military pensions were six times more lucrative than their counterparts in the private sector. Civil service retirees receive three times the benefits of those who work in the private sector. The commission also found that if these two federal benefits were brought in line with the private sector, the federal budget would save $58 billion over three years.

Pensions also last a significant time. An article by Pete Earley entitled "Inside the Veterans Administration," in the January 18, 1983, issue of the *Washington Post,* reports that the Veterans Administration was still paying 41 widows of Civil War veterans, 26 widows of Indian War veterans and 9182 widows of Spanish-American War veterans.

The Four Myths of the Elderly: White Paper from the American Association of Working People
"The Four Myths of the Elderly" is largely based on an article by Peter G. Peterson — "Social Security: I. The Coming Crash" and "II. A Plan for Salvation" — in the *New York Review of Books* (December 2 and December 16, 1982).

In addition, the following works were instrumental in the development of the argument I present in this section:

Buckley, William F. "Social Security: Reagan vs. Santa Claus" (*Rocky Mountain News,* October 15, 1984).

Demkovich, Linda E. "Budget Cutters Think the Unthinkable — Social Security Cuts Would Stem Red Ink" (*National Journal,* June 23, 1984).

Munnell, Alicia H. "A Calmer Look at Social Security" (*New York Review of Books,* March 17, 1983).

———. "The Current Status of Social Security Financing" (*New England Economic Review,* Federal Reserve Bank of Boston, May/June, 1983).

Peterson, Peter G. "A Reply to the Critics" (*New York Review of Books,* March 17, 1983).

"Report of the National Commission on Social Security Reform," January 1983. Superintendent of Documents, U.S. Government Printing Office, Washington, D.C. 20402.

Rinder, Rosemary. "We Can Afford to Support the Elderly" (*New York Review of Books,* March 17, 1983).

Skaperdas, Peter D., and James R. Capra. "The Social Security System After the 1983 Amendments," a Federal Reserve

Bank of New York unpublished report (does not represent views of the Federal Reserve System).

"Social Security Freeze" (*U.S. News & World Report,* January 28, 1985).

Svahn, John A., and Mary Ross. "Social Security Amendments of 1983: Legislative History and Summary of Provisions" (*Social Security Bulletin,* Vol. 46, no. 7, July 1983).

"The World Crisis in Social Security" (*The Futurist,* February 1983).

The figure of $7 trillion of unfunded liabilities, which appears at the end of this section, is a 1984 figure. It is not projected forward.

Immigration and Integration

Why We Closed Our Borders:
A Speech to the United Nations General Assembly by the Deputy
Secretary of State

My own book on immigration called *The Immigration Bomb,* written with co-author Gary Imhoff, will be published by E.P. Dutton, New York. A summary article on immigration is Georges Fauriol's "U.S. Immigration Policy and the National Interest" (*The Humanist,* May/June 1984).

Much valuable material is available from the Federation for American Immigration Reform (FAIR), 1424 16th Street N.W., Room 701, Washington, D.C. 20036. See, for instance, Roger Conner's pamphlet "Breaking Down the Barriers: The Changing Relationship Between Illegal Immigration and Welfare" (Federation for American Immigration Reform, September 1982).

Robert Fox's "The Challenge of Numbers" (*IDB News,* Interamerican Development Bank, Washington, D.C., December 1983), has some useful statistics on immigration and refugees. "Los Bandidos Take the Town: Castro's Outcasts Shoot Up New York," by Michael Daly (*New York,* October 1, 1980), gives some good statistics on the impact of immigration on crime. "The Impact of Immigration on U.S. Population Size," by Leon F. Bouvier (Population Reference Bureau), is the first in a series of occasional papers, "Population Trends in Public Policy." Two relevant articles appear in *Foreign Affairs:* "Coping with Illegal Immigrants," by Sylvia Anne Hewlett (Winter 1981–1982), and "Right vs. Right," by Michael S. Teitelbaum (Fall 1980). Two articles on the rise of Spanish-speaking Americans are "The Latinization of America," by Thomas B. Morgan (*Esquire,* May 1983), and "English, Si, Spanish, No," by Gregg Easterbrook (*Washington Monthly,* December 1980).

A more hopeful book on immigration is John Crendson's *The Tarnished Door* (Times Books, New York, 1984). See also Robert B. Reich's "Pie-slicers vs. Pie-enlargers" (*Washington Monthly,* September 1980).

Other relevant publications include "The Economic Implications of Immigration," by Kyle Johnson and James Orr (U.S. Department of Labor, Bureau of Labor Affairs, Office of Foreign Economic Research, July 15, 1980), and "Immigration Policies and Black America: Causes and Consequences" (proceedings before the seminar cosponsored by the Department of Human Development, School of Human Ecology, Howard University, and the Federation for American Immigration Reform, November 3, 1983). See also F. Ray Marshall, "Illegal Immigration: The Problem, the Solutions" (Federation for American Immigration Reform, Washington, D.C., August 1982).

The statistics on how many people guard the border and the future labor force in the developing world are from Michael S. Teitelbaum's "Right vs. Right: Immigration and Refugee Policy in the United States" (*Foreign Affairs,* Fall 1980). Statistics on the use of social services by illegal aliens are from Roger Conner's "Breaking Down the Barriers: The Changing Relationship Be-

tween Illegal Immigration and Welfare" (Federation for American Immigration Reform, September 1982).
See also:
Boulding, Kenneth E. "Toward a Twentieth Century Politics" (*Colorado Quarterly*, Summer 1976).
Dolman, Geoffrey, Jr., and Norman S. Kaufman. "Changing Demographics of Southwestern States: Colorado," a report prepared by the WICHE (Western Interstate Commission on Higher Education) Information Clearinghouse in cooperation with the Western Regional Office of the College Board.
"Public Opinion on Immigration," a pamphlet published by the Federation for American Immigration Reform (FAIR), 1424 16th Street N.W., Room 701, Washington, D.C. 20036.
"The Southwest — The Population Connection" (*The Other Side*, newsletter published by the Environmental Fund, No. 37, May/June 1984).

The Unmelted Pot: Report of the U.S. Civil Rights Commission
and
Children Having Children: Report of the U.S. Civil Rights Commission
See Neal Peirce, "Target: Fatherless Family Teenage Birth Problem" (*Denver Post*, April 18, 1983). "The Children of Children" by Ken Auletta (*Parade*, June 17, 1984) is a good description of dependency and poverty, as is "America's Fragmented Black Families, Helping Them Rebuild" (*Christian Science Monitor*, July 11, 1984). A monograph published by the Joint Center for Political Studies, Washington, D.C., in 1983, "A Policy Framework for Racial Justice," edited by Kenneth Clark, contains some statistics on the black family. See also Anne Hurlbert's "Children as Parents" (*New Republic*, September 10, 1985).

The statistics on black births are current statistics, and I assumed for this chapter that current trends would continue until the year 2000.

Crime and Terrorism

The Violent Decade:
Report of the President's Commission on Violence and Terrorism
What law enforcement will look like in the year 2000 is speculated upon in *Centurion Magazine.* See, for instance, "The Twenty-first Century Cop" (Vol. 2, no. 3, April 1984).

On crime and minorities see *America Now* by Marvin Harris (Simon & Schuster, New York, 1981), particularly the chapter "Why There's Terror on the Streets." The U.S. National Criminal Justice Information and Statistical Service publishes material every year that gives crime and race statistics. See also: "Street Gangs No Longer Just a Big City Problem" (*U.S. News & World Report,* July 16, 1984); Michael Hindgeland's "Race and Involvement in Common Law, Personal Crimes" (*American Sociological Review,* Vol. 43, 1978, pp. 93–109); and "Violent Death Rate of 50,000 a Year Cited as U.S. Health Concern" (*New York Times,* November 28, 1984).

The 1983 *Report to the Nation on Crime and Justice* from the Bureau of Justice Statistics, Department of Justice, says that in 1981, approximately 2.87 percent of the U.S. black population was arrested and approximately 0.75 percent of the U.S. white population was arrested. There have been no comparable statistics to the President's Commission on the Causes of Crime and the Prevention of Violence, but the 1983 *Source Book of Criminal Justice Statistics,* from the Bureau of Justice Statistics, says that in all cities in the United States, blacks account for 56 percent of those arrested for homicide, 54 percent of those arrested for rape, 63 percent for robbery, and 41 percent for assault. The 1981 FBI Crime Report states that blacks account for 12 percent of the U.S. population but 46 percent of arrests for violent crime and 31 percent of arrests for crimes against property.

On terrorism see "International Terrorism, Europe" and "Terrorism's Targets: Democracy, Israel and Jews," two special reports published by the Anti-Defamation League of B'nai B'rith. They also have a disturbing book, *Hate Groups in America: A Record of Bigotry and Violence,* published in 1981. The Fall 1982 issue of *Stanford Magazine* includes "The Deadly Game of Terrorism," by Derrell M. Trent. See also "Rash of Terrorism Ahead — Is U.S. Ready?" (*U. S. News & World Report,* July 16, 1984). Jenny Seper's "Extremists Can Get Explosives in West with Little Difficulty" (*The Arizona Republic,* April 8, 1984) is part of a series of articles on terrorism. "Euroterrorism in the '80s," by Gary Yerky (*Christian Science Monitor,* January 25, 1985), contains many important statistics.

Statistics on the PLO actions are from a special report, "P.L.O. and Arab Terrorism: A Decade of Violence," published in January 1979 by the Anti-Defamation League of B'nai B'rith.

Memorandum to the President from the Director of the Bureau of Prisons
This memorandum is based on "Prisonia 1990: The Future of the Nation?," a speech by Diana R. Gordon, President of the National Council on Crime and Delinquency, given November 11, 1981, at the Tenth Anniversary Conference of the Kansas Conference on Crime and Delinquency. In the speech she credits William Nagel, a former warden, with the original concept of Prisonia.

Breakdown

The Death of the American City: Special Report from the Department of Housing and Urban Development
Richard Louv's *America II* (Houghton Mifflin, Boston, 1983) and Michael C. D. MacDonald's *America's Cities* (Simon & Schuster,

New York, 1984) are valuable, as is Jane Jacobs's *Cities and the Wealth of Nations: Principles of Economic Life* (Random House, New York, 1984). See also "Urban Expert Warns Against Development of 'Two New Yorks,'" by Victoria Irwin (*Christian Science Monitor*, October 12, 1984); "America's Urban 'Rust Belt' Cinches Up For the Future," by Lucia Movat (*Christian Science Monitor*, May 25, 1984); and "Our Big Cities Go Ethnic," by William A. Chaze (*U.S. News & World Report*, March 21, 1983).

Report from the Commissioner of the Internal Revenue Service
The subject of Internal Revenue Service tax reform was much in the news while I was preparing this book, and my sources were entirely from articles on tax reform. See, for instance, "Tax Tangles" (*New Republic*, August 27, 1984) and "A Myriad of Individual Effects," by Gary Klott (*New York Times*, November 28, 1984), as well as numerous articles that appeared in the *Washington Post* and the *Wall Street Journal* on the same date, November 28, 1984. "Tax Reform for Fairness, Simplicity and Economic Growth," the Treasury Department's Report to the President, contains the justification for the Reagan proposal. "Business Will Bear the Brunt," by Anne Reilly (*Fortune*, November 26, 1984), and "Fair Share?" (*Wall Street Journal*, November 20, 1984) consider critiques of the various proposals, as does "Businessmen Hoist Warning Flags over Tax Simplification," by David T. Cook (*Christian Science Monitor*, November 20, 1984). "Tax Debate: Wide Issues," by Peter T. Kilborn (*New York Times*, September 24, 1984), and "The Tax Package That Can Save the Next President," by Kevin Phillips (*Washington Post National Weekly*, August 13, 1984), contain critical viewpoints. "Tax Revision: Political Paydirt," by Thomas B. Edsall (*Washington Post National Weekly*, January 28, 1985), furnished some material. Another viewpoint can be obtained from an op-ed piece, "Tax Reform Is Not Apple Pie," by John H. Makin (*Christian Science Monitor*, February 26, 1985).

Memorandum to the President from the Attorney General
Choosing a President, 1980, by the League of Women Voters Education Fund, Washington, D.C., contains some very good material on the electoral college system.

See also "The Electoral College — Why It Ought to Be Abolished," 37 *Fordham Law Review* 1 (1968); "One Man, 3,312 Votes: A Mathematical Analysis of the Electoral College," 13 *Villanova Law Review* 303 (Winter 1968).

PAC Man-Report of the U.S. Election Commission
See the various publications of Common Cause, especially "People Against PACs: A Common Cause Guide to Winning the War Against Political Action" (1984). "PACs: Too Big for Their Own Good," by Michael Wing and Robert L. Jackson, appeared in the *Los Angeles Times,* June 14, 1984. "Realtor, Doctor PACs Show Clout" (*Wall Street Journal,* November 6, 1984) shows some of the effect of PACs on the 1984 election, as does "PAC Money Talks Louder Now," by Brooks Jackson (*Wall Street Journal,* December 4, 1984). "Eruption of PACs Subsides as Political Phenomenon Matures," by Peter Grier (*Christian Science Monitor,* January 7, 1985), and "The Political Goldrush Gathers Speed" (*U. S. News & World Report,* December 17, 1984) also have some good material on this important matter.

Poisoning America-National Academy of Sciences Report
Samuel S. Epstein, Lester O. Brown, and Carl Pope provide a comprehensive review of this area in *Hazardous Waste in America* (Sierra Club Books, San Francisco, 1982). "Finding the Bad Actors in a World of Chemicals," by Pepper Leaper (*The News Report,* Vol. 34, no. 3, March 1984, published by The National Academy of Sciences), also contains some important material, as

do "Environmental Quality, 1982" and similar reports by the Council on Environmental Quality.

By the end of 1981, there were 5,566,102 chemicals on the registry of chemicals maintained by the American Chemical Society. See Fred Powledge's *Water* (Farrar, Straus & Giroux, New York, 1982).

The Environmental Protection Agency estimates that in 1977, only 10 percent of the toxic and hazardous materials were being disposed of safely. See Powledge's *Water*.

Education

Report Card on American Education from the Secretary of Education
Numerous publications on education came out during the preparation of this book, of which "A Nation at Risk" by the National Commission on Excellence in Education (April 1983) was one of the best. A special report on education in the August 28, 1984, *Christian Science Monitor,* "Now Johnny Has to Read," was helpful, as was an education survey by the *New York Times,* "Improving Our Teachers" (January 6, 1985). "A Call for Action" is a report issued by the Governor's Task Force on Education for Economic Growth in Delaware. "Can the Schools Be Saved?" in the May 9, 1983, issue of *Newsweek* and "U.S. Pupils Lag from Grade One, Study Finds," in the August 17, 1984, *New York Times,* show how far behind other students American students are. The Education Commission of the States, created in 1965 as an interstate compact to help state political and education leaders improve the quality of education, has numerous publications, available from Education Commission of the States, 1860 Lincoln Street, Denver, Colorado 80295. One of them, published in the latter part of 1984, is a summary of the major recommendations of the

major reports on education. The Congressional Research Service of the Library of Congress published "Comparison of Recommendations from Selected Education Commission Reports" in 1984. *Vital Speeches of the Day* for June 15, 1984, contains "A 'Notion' at Risk," by Jeffrey R. Holland, president of Brigham Young University, a speech that he gave to the National Press Club, Washington, D.C., March 22, 1984.

Other major books on education include books concerned with the high schools: *High School,* by Ernest L. Boyer (Harper & Row, New York, 1983); *The Good High School: Portraits of Character and Culture,* by Sara L. Lightfoot (Basic Books, New York, 1983); and *Horace's Compromise: The Dilemma of the American High School,* by Theodore R. Sizer (Houghton Mifflin, Boston, 1984).

A Place Called School, by John Goodlad (McGraw-Hill, New York, 1984), is a general book on schools.

On teachers and teaching, see Ken Macrorie, *Twenty Teachers* (Oxford University Press, New York, 1984); "A Call for Change in Teacher Education," Report of the National Commission for Excellence in Teacher Education, Washington, D.C., 1985; and Lee S. Shulman and Gary Sykes, *Handbook of Teaching and Policy* (Longman, New York, 1983).

On the impacts of computers on education, see Seymour Papert, *Mindstorms: Children, Computers and Powerful Ideas* (Basic Books, New York, 1982).

On educational change and the future, see Michael Fullan, *The Meaning of Educational Change* (Teachers College Press, New York, 1982); and Alvin Toffler, *The Third Wave* (Morrow, New York, 1980).

Harold W. Stevenson argues in "Making the Grade: School Advancement in Japan, Taiwan and the United States" (*1983 Annual Report of the Center for Advanced Study in the Behavioral Sciences,* Stanford University) that U.S. education holds up "too small a mirror" to evaluate our educational system. He finds "although a small proportion of American children perform superbly, the large majority appear to be falling further and further behind their peers in other countries."

I used various sources in preparing the section titled "The Dark Ages of Higher Education." John D. Millett's *Conflict in Higher Education* (Jossey-Bass, San Francisco, 1984) examines the current status of higher education. I very much enjoyed an article by Chester E. Finn, Jr., called "Trying Higher Education: An Eight-count Indictment" (*Change Magazine,* May–June 1984). The recent report of the Association of American Colleges Project in Redefining the Meaning and Purpose of Baccalaureate Degrees (see *The Chronicle of Higher Education,* February 13, 1985) is a thorough critique of higher education.

See also David Breneman, "Higher Education and the Economy" (*Educational Record,* Vol. 62, no. 2, Spring 1981); James R. Mingle et al., *Challenges of Retrenchment* (Jossey-Bass, San Francisco, 1981); "In Pursuit of Excellence," the Report of the Pritchard Committee on Higher Education in Kentucky's Future, 1981 (published by the Council on Higher Education, West Frankfort Office Complex, Frankfort, Kentucky 40601); and the Carnegie Council on Policy Studies in Higher Education, *Three Thousand Futures: The Next Twenty Years for Higher Education* (Jossey-Bass, San Francisco, 1980).

Law and Lawyers

Statement of the Chief Justice of the Supreme Court to the Senate Judiciary Committee

Jethro K. Lieberman's *The Litigious Society* (Basic Books, New York, 1981) is a useful book on the legal system. Numerous articles have appeared on this subject. See "Lawyers Versus the Marketplace," by Richard Greene (*Forbes,* January 16, 1984); "Law by the Numbers," by Richard Greene (*Forbes,* January 30, 1984); "Soaring Legal Costs: Even Lawyers Are Worried" (*U.S.*

News & World Report, August 13, 1984); "Burger Urges Lawyers to Polish Ethics, Help Unclog Courts" (*Christian Science Monitor,* February 13, 1984); "Too Many Lawyers: Too Much Law?" by Shirley M. Hufstedler (*Bar Leader Magazine,* July-August 1984); "The U. S. May Finally Have Too Many Lawyers" (*Business Week,* September 17, 1984); "American Legal Education: A Form of Brain Damage" by Arthur S. Miller (*Miami Herald,* September 2, 1984); "Adding Insult to Injury," by Teresa Riordan (*Washington Monthly,* March 1984); "Fat Fees" (*Time,* July 27, 1981); "Why Lawyers Are in the Doghouse" (*U.S. News & World Report,* May 11, 1981); "The Trouble with Lawyers," by Charles Fried (*New York Times Magazine,* February 12, 1984); "Reflections upon Law and Lawyers" (*Harvard Law School Bulletin,* Winter 1984); "Loser Pays Nothing," by Richard Neeley (*Washington Monthly,* June 1983); "Puncturing Three Myths About Litigation," by John W. Cooley (*American Bar Association Journal,* December 1984). A paper on lawyer demographics was presented by Barbara A. Curran, associate executive director of the American Bar Association, to the August 1982 meeting of the American Bar Association in New Orleans, Louisiana.

International Traumas

Memorandum to the President from the Secretary of Agriculture
and
The Sin of Softheartedness: A Sermon by the Right Rev. Robert King
The statistics on Africa are from "Famine, a Race Against Time," by Michael Hanlon (*World Press Review,* February 1985). Other sources include "Africa's Food Crisis Has Deep Century-old Roots," by Richard Critchfield (*Christian Science Monitor,* June 6, 1984); "Africa Offers Foreign Policy Plusses for Reagan," by

David Winder (*Christian Science Monitor,* May 14, 1984); "The Anguish of Africa," by Geoffrey Wheatcroft (*New Republic,* January 9 and 16, 1983); "A Continent Gone Wrong" (*Time* magazine, January 16, 1984); "Seeds of Revolution," by David K. Willis (*Christian Science Monitor,* November 28, 1984); "Prescription for Change," by David K. Willis (*Christian Science Monitor,* November 29, 1984); "What Can You Do to Help?," by David K. Willis (*Christian Science Monitor,* November 30, 1984); "If Compassion Fades, More Africans Will Die," by John Richardson (*Christian Science Monitor,* November 30, 1984); "Can Monetary Aid Alter African Economics?" by David R. Francis (*Christian Science Monitor,* October 11, 1984); "Gentle Rains Feed Africa's Hopes," by Paul Van Slambrock (*Christian Science Monitor,* December 20, 1984); "Africa's Tests Harder Than Job's" (*Denver Post,* December 28, 1984); "Evidence Suggests Africa's Drought Is Here to Stay," by Robert C. Cowen (*Christian Science Monitor,* February 14, 1985).

I am indebted to my friend Garrett Hardin, whose *Naked Emperors: Essays of a Taboo Stalker* (William Kaufman, Los Altos, Calif., 1982) was important to my thinking and that of many others. The theme of softheartedness is expounded in his article "The Immorality of Being Softhearted" (*Stanford Alumni Almanac,* January 1969). The concept of "toughlove" came from Garrett Hardin, as did the idea of comparing the developing histories of India and China. Edgar R. Chasteen's book, *The Case for Compulsory Birth Control* (Prentice-Hall, Englewood Cliffs, N.J., 1972), will offend everyone and thus deserves to be read. The John McPhee quote comes from *Encounters with the Archdruid* (Farrar, Straus & Giroux, New York, 1971). The Joseph Townsend quote is from *A Dissertation on the Poor Laws, by a Wellwisher of Mankind,* by Joseph Townsend (University of California Press, Berkeley, 1971).

A series that appeared in the *Boston Globe,* "Population Straining the Limits," was published as a separate monograph by that newspaper in 1982. Pertinent statistics are contained in "Mexico, the City Unlimited," by Fred Pearce (*The New Science,* October 18, 1984); "People, People, People" (*Time,* August 6, 1984); "A

Proud Capital's Distress" (*Time,* August 6, 1984); and "The Population Debate" (*World Press Review,* October 1984). See also a series in the *Christian Science Monitor,* "People Versus Resources," by David K. Willis (August 6, 1984), and "Malthusian Time Bomb Still Ticking," by Richard Bernstein (*New York Times,* July 29, 1984). An unpublished paper, "Population Growth: Its Implications for Third World Stability and International Security," by Marshall Green of the Population Crisis Committee, sets forth the stakes in this area. See also "McNamara's Time Bomb or Myth: The Population Problem" (*Foreign Affairs,* Summer 1984) and *Human Numbers, Human Needs,* by Paul Harrison and John Rowley (International Planned Parenthood Federation, London, 1984).

State of the World, 1984, by Lester Brown et al. (World Watch Institute, New York, 1984), states a strong case for population outrunning food. See also "World Population Growth, Soil Erosion and Food Security" by Lester Brown (*Science,* November 1981); *Agriculture 2000 — A Look at the Future* (Battelle Press, Columbus, Ohio, 1984); and "Green Revolution Hits Double Trouble" (*U.S. News & World Report,* July 28, 1980).

For the moral issues involved, see a stimulating dialogue in *Social Ethics,* by Thomas Mappes and Jane Sembaty (McGraw-Hill, New York, 1977).

On our shrinking agricultural base, see the series by Harlan C. Clifford that appeared in the *Christian Science Monitor,* July 31, August 15, and September 5, 1984. A classic book, *Topsoil and Civilization,* by Vernon Gil Carter and Tom Dale (University of Oklahoma Press, Norman, 1948), contains some magnificent language on the relationship of agriculture, topsoil, and civilization. "Bitter Harvest" (*Time,* October 4, 1982) well describes some of the American farming dilemmas. The question of American agricultural resources, particularly soil, is addressed by Jonathan Harsh in the *Christian Science Monitor* in "Soil, the Crucial Resource" (September 13, 1982); a second article appeared September 14, 1982; he explored the same theme in "Are American Farmers Exporting Their Topsoil?" (*Christian Science Monitor,* June 3, 1981).

Information on Egypt is found in "Egypt's Identity Crisis" (*World Press Review,* November 1984).

Memorandum to the President from the Secretary of State
A book on the resource war is Bohdan O. Szuprowicz's *Strategic Material Shortages: Dealing with Cartels, Embargoes and Supply Disruptions* (John Wiley & Sons, New York, 1981). Also see "The Next U.S. Crisis Will Be Minerals and Metals" (*Government Executive,* October 1980). Richard Nixon's *The Real War* (Warner Books, New York, 1980) is worth reading. Dated, but still worthwhile, is "Population and Resources: The Coming Collision" (*Population Bulletin,* a publication of the Population Reference Bureau, Vol. 26, no. 2, June 1970). See also "Will the U.S. Be Left Vulnerable if a 'Resource War' Breaks Out?" by Michael Gordon (*National Journal,* April 18, 1981); "Outmoded Assumptions," by Henry Steele Commager (*The Atlantic,* March 1982).

The table on U.S. import dependence comes from a white paper, "The Resource War and the U.S. Business Community: The Case for a Council on Economics and National Security," published by the Council on Economics and National Security (CENS), Suite 601, 1730 Rhode Island Avenue N.W., Washington, D.C. 20036, with a date of first printing June 1980, second revised printing August 1980. A similar table is found in Michael Gordon's "Will the U.S. Be Left Vulnerable if a 'Resource War' Breaks Out?," in *The National Journal* (April 18, 1981), and the subject is also dealt with in "Elements of a National Materials Policy," A Report of the National Research Council of the National Academy of Sciences National Materials Advisory Board, dated August 1972 in publication NMAB 294 by the National Academy of Sciences, National Academy of Engineering, 2101 Constitution Avenue, Washington, D.C. 20418.

Crisis: Problems Outrunning Solutions

Letter of Resignation of the Secretary of Energy
Though I go into very few energy statistics, a useful reference is
U.S. Energy Policies, by Don Kash and Robert W. Rycroft (University of Oklahoma Press, Norman, 1984); also see "Oil and the Decline of the West," by Walter J. Levy (*Foreign Affairs,* Summer 1980). "The Geopolitics of Oil," a staff report of the Committee on Energy and Natural Resources (December 1980), is also helpful.

Memorandum to the President from the Commanding Officer, U.S.
Army Corps of Engineers
For background information on the current and anticipated water shortage see:

Brown, Lester R. *State of the World: A Worldwatch Institute Report on Progress Toward a Sustainable Society* (W.W. Norton, New York, 1984).

Kelso, Maurice M.; Martin, William E.; Mack, Lawrence E. "Water Supplies and Economic Growth in an Arid Environment: An Arizona Case Study" (University of Arizona Press, Tucson, 1973).

Water-Related Technologies for Sustainable Agriculture in U.S. Arid/ Semiarid Lands (U.S. Congress, Office of Technology Assessment, OTA-F-212, Washington, D.C., October 1983).

"Water Outlook: As Uncertain as the Weather" (Conservation Foundation Letter, April 1977).

Wilson, James. *Ground Water: A Non-Technical Guide* (Academy of Natural Sciences, Philadelphia, 1982).

Memorandum to the President from the Secretary of Labor
The Work Revolution, by Gail Schwartz (Rawson Associates, New York, 1983), addresses the question of labor and the coming job drought. John Naisbitt, in *Megatrends* (Warner Books, New York, 1982), takes the exact opposite viewpoint and argues that there will be a labor shortage in the future.

"Storm Clouds on the Horizon," by Barry Bluestone, Bennett Harrison, and Lucy Gorham (Economic Education Project, 152 Aspinall Ave., Suite 2, Brookline, Mass. 02146), gives the following history of average unemployment rates during the tenure of American Presidents since World War II:

Truman (1946–52)	4.2%
Eisenhower (1953–60)	4.9%
Kennedy/Johnson (1961–68)	4.9%
Nixon/Ford (1969–75)	5.8%
Carter (1977–80)	6.5%
Reagan (1981–83)	8.9%

See also the symposium "Do We Need an Industrial Policy?" (*Harper's,* February 1985). A pamphlet, "The Learning Enterprise," by Lewis J. Perelman (Council of State Planning Agencies, 400 North Capitol Street, Washington, D.C. 20001), describes the structural transformation of the world economy and the educational alternatives.

Memorandum to the President from the Chief of the Forest Service
An overview of this problem is found in "An Introduction to the World Conservation Strategy," prepared by the Commission on Education of the International Union for Conservation of Nature and Natural Resources and published by the United Nations Environment Program (1984). See also Eric Eckholm, "Planting for the Future: Forestry for Human Needs" (Worldwatch Paper No. 26, Worldwatch Institute, Washington, D.C., February 1979);

Peter T. White, "Tropical Rainforests: Nature's Dwindling Treasures" (*National Geographic,* Vol. 163, no. 1, January 1983); and Paul and Anne Ehrlich, *Extinction: The Causes and Consequences of the Disappearance of Species* (Random House, New York, 1981).

"Are Deserts on the March?" by John Carey (*International Wildlife,* March-April 1985) gives figures on areas desertified by man. The United Nations Environment Program is cited as estimating that 3 billion hectares (11.5 million square miles) has been desertified by man. That is an area as large as North and South America combined.

"The Rain Forests," by Catherine Caufield (*The New Yorker,* January 14, 1985), is a comprehensive article.

Other useful sources include:

Allen, Robert. *How to Save the World: Strategy for World Conservation* (Kogan Page, London, 1980).

Biological Diversity. Council on Environmental Quality, U.S. Government Printing Office, 1980.

Firor, John. "Interconnections in the 'Endangered Species' of the Atmosphere," *Journal '84,* World Resources Institute, 1984.

Johnson, A. H., and R. I. Bruck. "Hypotheses Linking Acidic Deposition and Other Airborne Pollutants to Forest Damage in the United States and Federal Republic of Germany," unpublished paper prepared for the U.S. Department of Energy, 1985.

Myers, Norman. *The Primary Source: Tropical Forests and Our Future* (W. W. Norton, New York, 1984).

Train, Russell. "Ecological Basis for Sustainable Development," *Journal '84,* World Resources Institute, 1984.

World Conservation Strategy: Living Resource Conservation for Sustainable Development, International Union for the Conservation of Nature and Natural Resources, Gland, Switzerland, and United Nations Environment Program, Nairobi, Kenya, 1980.

One difficulty in writing from the perspective of the year 2000 is what numbers to use. The numbers given in this memorandum are 1985 numbers, with these exceptions: In 1985 there were 800 million landless people in the rural areas of the Third World. I increased the number to 1.2 billion for a year 2000 equivalent. The 1985 estimate is that by the year 2000, 2.3 billion people will have trouble finding adequate fuel supplies and that 350 million will not have wood for their minimum needs. I assumed the projection. The global consumption of industrial wood is projected to double by the year 2000 and I assumed the projection, as I did with the global demand for paper products. The figure for the decline in forests in the Federal Republic of Germany is 51.8 percent in 1984. I projected the 70 percent figure. It climbed from 34 percent in 1983 to 51 percent in 1984, so the estimate is probably low. The estimated amount of carbon dioxide released by burning felled timber is 2 to 4 billion tons, and it is estimated that it will increase four times by the year 2000.

The current rate of extinction of species is 1000 a year, and the year 2000 rate is projected to be 10,000 a year.

Memorandum to the President from the Comptroller of the Currency
See "The Debt Bomb: A Web of Peril," by Janez Stanovnik (*World Press Review*, August 1984); "Debtor's Decision" (*The Economist*, June 16, 1984); "The Debt Bomb Ticks," an editorial (*New York Times*, March 21, 1984); "World Debt Maladies Ease a Bit but Are Seen Lingering on for Years," by Art Pine (*Wall Street Journal*, November 25, 1983); "The Dynamite Issue," by David Pauley et al. (*Newsweek*, May 30, 1983); "Nations in Debt Try to Pull Themselves Back from the Brink," by David R. Francis (*Christian Science Monitor*, February 27, 1984); and "Our Fragile Banking System," by John M. Berry (*Washington Post National Weekly*, June 11, 1984). Recently, numerous commentators have pointed out that the problem has gotten considerably better over the last year. See, for example, "World 'Debt' Bomb Nearly Defused," by David Warsh (*Boston Globe*, February 19, 1985), and "Third World Debt: The Bomb Is Defused," by Gary Hector (*Fortune*, February 18, 1985).

A good article on the income redistribution in the Third World is "Third World, All but the Rich Are Poorer" (*Los Angeles Times*, November 4, 1984).

The quote from Lord Lever, chairman of the Commonwealth Export Group on Developing Countries' External Debt Problem, is from *The Baxter Newsletter*, September 14, 1984, Bulletin 37, "The Next Banking Crisis."

Forgotten Fundamentals of Public Policy: Speech by the Administrator of the Environmental Protection Agency to the National Education Association

In writing this section I relied almost entirely upon "The Forgotten Fundamentals of the Energy Crisis," by Albert A. Bartlett of the Department of Physics and Astrophysics at the University of Colorado, Boulder. This paper was originally given to the Third Annual Conference on Energy (University of Missouri at Rolla, October 12–14, 1976) and a later version appeared in the *American Journal of Physics* (September 1978). I am most grateful to Dr. Bartlett for permission to use his ideas.

The mushroom story is from Kirkpatrick Sale's *Human Scale* (Coward, McCann, and Geoghegan, New York, 1980).

Part II: Copernican Politics

The Morgenstern Years

It is difficult to cite the specific references from a lifetime of reading and years of experience that provided me with the material with which to write "The Morgenstern Years." However, the titles listed below made significant contributions to my thinking.

On the federal deficit: The figure for the amount of money that the Reagan administration has contributed to the federal deficit was obtained from "The Economic and Budget Outlook: Fiscal Years 1986–1990," Part I of a Report to the Senate and House Committees on the Budget, Congressional Budget Office, February 6, 1985.

On leadership:

Bennis, Dr. Warren, and Burt Nanus. *Leaders: The Strategies for Taking Charge* (New York: Harper & Row, 1985).

Fairlie, Henry. "The Politician's Art" (*Harper's*, December 1977).

Greenfield, Meg. "Our No-Good Presidents" (*Newsweek*, November 28, 1983).

Peirce, Neal R. "Politics and Politicians in a Winter of Discontent" (*Denver Post*, December 21, 1975).

Reeves, Richard. "The Leadership Quagmire" (*Esquire*, December 1979).

Saikowski, Charlotte. "Does the American Presidency Work?" (*Christian Science Monitor*, June 5, 1984).

"Thinking Through Leadership" (*Saturday Review/World*, November 16, 1974).

Zaleznik, Abraham. "Managers and Leaders: Are They Different?" (*Harvard Business Review*, May/June 1977).

On population:

Gupte, Pranay. *The Crowded Earth* (W. W. Norton, New York, 1984).

McDowell, Bart, and Stephanie Maze. "Mexico City: An Alarming Giant," and Robert Fox, "The Urban Explosion," both from *National Geographic*, August 1984, pp. 138–86.

McNamara, Robert. "Time Bomb or Myth: the Population Problem" (*Foreign Affairs*, Summer 1984).

Piotrow, Phyllis T. "World Population, the Present and Future Crisis" (Headline Series 251, Foreign Policy Association, New York).

Willis, David K. A major five-part series on world population (*Christian Science Monitor,* August 6–13, 1984).

Part III: The Time of Peace

I am very grateful to my friend John G. Stoessinger and his book *Why Nations Go to War* (St. Martin's Press, New York, 1982), which is an important contribution to peace.

Index

Haiti, immigrants from, 68, 71
Hazardous wastes, 111–114; costs
  for, 113, 117; and groundwater,
  114–116
Health care: for black pregnant
  teens, 79, 80; cost of, 20, 36–39,
  42–43, 212; "cost effectiveness" of,
  46; as "disease cure," 41, 47; egalitarian revolution in, 37; and elderly, 53–54; and hazardous wastes,
  117; inefficiency of, 37, 39–41,
  212, 213–214, 244; and life expectancy, 39; misallocation in, 47; and
  Morgenstern years, 211–216,
  218–219, 228; vs. public health im-
  provements, 214; rationing of, 36,
  39, 43–44; and transplanted/
  artificial organs, 40–41, 44–48; and
  terminally ill, 41–42, 43, 214; for
  veterans, 59–60. See also Medicaid;
  Medicare; Public health
Heilbroner, Robert L., on Third
  World poverty, 141
Helmer, Olaf, on forecasting, 97
Helms, Jesse, 199
Herostratos, and terrorism, 90–91
High-tech industries: employment in,
  9, 165; and middle class disappearance, 28–29; and unemployment,
  165
Hispanic Quebec, 69, 74, 76
Hispanics: "Aztlan" nation demanded by, 75–76; crime by, 88;
  education of, 78, 121; and immigration, 4, 69–70, 74–75; and
  prison population, 94. See also Minorities
Historical analogies: Athenian
  freedom, 84; Roman lead
  poisoning, 111; Roman taxation,
  105
History: civilizations' rise and fall in,
  16, 198; failure to learn from, 153;
  Gibbon on, 191–192; peace in,
  235; and political genius, 197; surprises of, 1–2
Hitler, Adolf, rise of, 199
Holmes, Oliver Wendell, Jr., on
  taxes, 103
Hong Kong: economic miracle in,
  183; trade exploitation by, 31

Huxley, Aldous, on facts, 72
Hyperinflation, 18

Illegitimacy, and black teenagers, 79,
  80
Illich, Ivan, on health care, 41
Illiteracy: in developing countries,
  226; in U.S., 120–121, 167
Immigration, 66–73; and American
  ideals, 68, 71, 73, 74, 221; failure
  to control, 22, 76–77; growth
  of, 67–68; Hispanic, 4, 69–71,
  74–75; limitation of, 66, 69, 71,
  73; and Morgenstern years,
  220–222, 229; and unemployment, 71, 76, 164–165, 221–
  222
Immigration and Nationality Act
  (1965), 69
Income, per capita or per worker:
  U.S. decline in, 15–16, 241; for
  U.S. vs. Mexico, 71
India: and foreign assistance, 148;
  forest loss in, 171, 175; labor force
  growth in, 163; nuclear war by,
  236–240; population of, 141
Industry: deterioration of, 3–4, 24,
  30–31; failure to invest in, 25–26;
  foreign competition for, 25; hazardous wastes from, 111–117;
  health care costs in, 37–38,
  211–212; shoddy goods from, 26;
  U.S. security in, 218. See also Economy; High-tech industry; Smokestack America
Inflation: from bank rescue, 181–182,
  183; geometric growth of, 187; hyperinflation, 18; and military pensions, 57; between 1967 and 2000,
  17; in 1970s, 196; and oil crisis,
  18; in Social Security assumption on,
  19
Inflation riots, 18
Integrative thinking. See Systems
  thinking
Interest rate: and Morgenstern years,
  203–204, 210; in 1991 banking crisis, 180–181, 182
Intergenerational conflict, 52–55; and
  Social Security, 19, 52–55, 62–63,
  64

Third World *(Cont.)*
163, 164; and Morgenstern aid
program, 223; and nuclear weapons, 93–94; population growth in,
224; poverty depicted in, 141–142;
selling of kidneys in, 45; triage
ethics for, 145, 147; unemployment in, 226
Third World debt, 16, 17, 180–181,
183–184; and Arab money, 18,
180, 182–183; and 1991 bank crisis, 181–182
Third World War: August 1985, The
(Hackett), vii
Time of Peace, 238, 241–242
Tocqueville, Alexis de, on democracy, 192
Topsoil: as American blessing, 197;
contamination of, 114; loss of, 23,
138, 139–140
Townsend, Joseph, 143
Toxic waste. *See* Hazardous wastes
Toynbee, Arnold: on death of civilizations, 131; on developed countries, 13; on freedom, 18; on institutions, 106
Trade, foreign: in agricultural products, 139; and international debt,
182; surplus to deficit in, 15; U.S.
exploited in, 25, 31–33; and U.S.
industrial decline, 3–4, 30–31
Trade deficit, 9, 24–27; and arms
cost, 241; and health costs, 38;
and Morgenstern years, 204–206,
207, 228; and petroleum taxation,
207
Triage ethics, 143–151
Tropical forests, 168, 169, 170
Truman, Harry, on leadership,
193

Underground economy, 103
Unemployment, 164–167; among
blacks, 89; and crime, 95; and deliberately idle, 22; and education,
121; in developing countries, 226;
and immigration, 71, 76, 164–165,
221–222; in Mexico, 70; Social Security assumption on, 19, 63–64;
and technology, 167; and trade

deficit, 205; worldwide rise of,
70
USSR. *See* Soviet Union

Veterans, increased numbers of, 54,
57. *See also* Military pensions
Veterans benefits, 59; cost of, 60;
and Morgenstern years, 208. *See
also* Entitlements
Vigilantism, rise of, 85
Villari, Pasquale, on greatness of nations, 65
Violence, 235; of 1990s, 84, 91–92;
in schools, 122. *See also* Crime; Racial and cultural conflict; Riots;
Terrorism
Vision, national, 15

Wallace, George, as independent
candidate, 108
Wall Street: computerized replace-
ment of, 101; as fortress city, 100
Washington, George, as leader, 193
Water: crisis in, 159–162; and forest
loss, 175; and groundwater contamination, 114–116; and 1990s
drought, 71
Wealth, national. *See* Economy; National wealth; Income, per capita
or per worker
Welfare load, international, 132–133;
in Africa, 133–135; in Argentina,
136–137; in Egypt, 135–136; need
to restrict, 132, 137, 140–142; and
triage ethics, 143–151. *See also* Foreign aid
Welfare system, and illegitimacy,
80–81
West Germany: doctors/life expectancy in, 39; forest decline in, 174;
lawyers in, 129
"White flight," 77, 101
Wilson, E. O., on species loss, 176
Wood, demand for, 172–173
World gross product, U.S. share in,
15. *See also* National wealth
World War I, and nuclear-war beginning, 94, 237

Zeno, on suicide, 50